Peregrination of Haryanvi Chhora

FROM THE BATTLEFIELDS TO THE SKIES

A Legacy of Valour
(From WW-I To Kargil)

THANKS GIVING

TO

INDIAN AIR FORCE

FROM THE BATTLEFIELDS TO THE SKIES

A Legacy of Valour

(From WW-I to Kargil)

Air Commodore Vijai Singh Yadav (V)

Foreword by

Air Marshal (Dr) L K Verma AVSM
MBBS, MSc Phd
Former DG Medical Services AF

PENTAGON PRESS LLP

First published in 2025 by
PENTAGON PRESS LLP
206, Peacock Lane, Shahpur Jat
New Delhi-110049, India
Contact: 011-26490600

Typeset in AGaramond, 11.5 Point
Printed at Aegean Offset Printers, Greater Noida

ISBN 978-81-993527-2-8

Disclaimer: The views and opinions expressed in the book is the individual assertion of the Author. The Publisher does not take any responsibility for the same in any manner whatsoever. The same shall solely be the responsibility of the Author.

www.pentagonpress.in

LORD KRISHNA

LORD KRISHNA
HIS MESSAGE, HIS *VARDAN*, HIS BLESSINGS TO THE *YADUVANSHI*

It is my proud privilege to mention that how blessed as *Yaduvanshi* we are! Even after the curse of Gandhari we have survived for millennia and maintained our purity under the protection of Lord Krishna. Anyone who takes refuge or *Sharan* with the *Yaduvanshi* attains an exalted state – free from sins. This is the *Vardan* (boon) to the *Yaduvanshi* for spreading the purity.

However, if the *Yaduvanshi* themselves begin to indulge in misdeeds/ untruthfulness, how can they spread the purity? By opening the gates of lust, greed, and anger we have contaminated/eroded the mind and corrupted the very idea of spreading purity.

The *Ahir* or *Yaduvanshi* are there to spread purity. Even *Shrimad Bhagwadgita* says so. Therefore, let us do away with worldly luxuries and get back to the wishes of God.

BHAGVATA PURANA

I shall describe to you the most pious ritual which takes away all the sins of men. A man who hears the descendants of the legendary King *Yadu* is freed from all sins. Where the Supreme Soul descends in human form, they were known as *Yadosa, Satrojit, Kroshta,* and *Nala Ripu.*

Thus, the *Yadu* dynasty is the most sacred one. It is the destroyer of all the sins of man. In this lineage, Lord Parabrahma himself had incarnated in the form of a human being who is called Lord Shri Krishna. The person who listens to the *Yaduvanshi* will be freed from all sins.

मैं तुम्हें सबसे पवित्र अनुष्ठान का वर्णन करूंगा जो मनुष्यों के सभी पापों को दूर कर देता है। जो मनुष्य यदुवंशियों की कथा सुनता है वह सभी पापों से मुक्त हो जाता है। जहां भगवान, परमात्मा, मानव रूप में अवतरित हुए। उन्हें यदोसा, सत्रोजीत, क्रोष्ठा और नाला रिपु के नाम से जाना जाता था।

(भागवत पुराण)

अर्थः यदु वंश परम पवित्र वंश है। यह मनुष्य के समस्त पापों को नष्ट करनेवाला है इस वंश में स्वयम भगवान परब्रह्म ने मनुष्य के रूप में अवतार लिया था जिन्हें श्रीकृष्ण कहते है। जो मनुष्य यदुवंश का श्रवण करेगा वह समस्त पापों से मुक्त हो जाएगा।

वर्णयामि महापुण्यं सर्वपापहरं नृणां। यदोर्वन्श नरः श्रुत्त्वा सर्वपापैः प्रमुच्यते। यत्र-अवतीर्णो भगवान् परमात्मा नराकृतिः । यदोसत्रोजित्क्रोष्ठा नलो रिपुरिति श्रुताः ।

(भागवत पुराण) 2

भावार्थः यदुवंशः पवित्रतमः वंशः अस्ति। मनुष्यस्य सर्वपापनाशनम्। अस्मिन् वंशे भगवान् परब्रह्म एव श्रीकृष्ण इति नाम्रा मानवरूपेण अवतार कृतवान् आसीत्। यदुवंशः श्रणोति सः सर्वपापैः मुक्तः भविष्यति। 142

The Bhagavad-Gita, contains the divine words emanation from the lips of God Himself whose glory is infinite, unlimited, and beyond simple description.

Thou art Mother, Thou art Father, Thou art Kinsman, Thou art Friends, Thou art Knowledge, Thou art Wealth, Thou art My All, O' Lord of Lords, Obeisance to Krishna, Guide and Teacher of the World, Son of Vasudeva, Chastiser of Kamsa and Canura, Charioteer of Arjuna and Devika's Supreme Delight.

Has given *Vardan*/Blessing to the *Yaduvansh*, let us honour it.

My message to the Yaduvanshi and its leaders.

* * *

"गमन लक्ष्यात् पथः सौन्दर्यम् पान्थे अधिकम्।"

JOURNEY IS MORE BEAUTIFUL THAN DESTINATION

* * *

AHIR REGIMENT

My Views

The Answers have changed, by Kishore Asthana.

Mr. Albert Einstein was teaching at the Oxford University, he gave his senior students an examination, later his assistance asked him why he had given the same examination given last year, because **the answers have changed.**

I am inspired by Mr Albert Einstein that the questions are the same but the answers have changed, the same demand for AHIR REGIMENT has been there for decades, during British Raj and subsequently by different government after independence, but now things have changed, we now have a person Mr Narender Bhai Modi head of a government who is the only one who takes hard decisions and makes impossible into possible, he therefore becomes our best bet.

It is proven fact the Ahirs without mentioning any wars or battles, their bravery and valour has been recognised by the British but when it came to sanction Ahir Regiment the British were unable to forget the 1857. (First War of Independence)

There has been several attempts for demand for an Ahir Regiment through small scale Andolan or through certain politician but never any serious thought given by any Government

Chaudhary Brahm Prakash when he was the Agriculture Minister in the late seventies wanted to meet my eldest brother Major General S D S Yadava when he learnt that my brother for becoming the first Ahir General. After the exchange of pleasantries my brother asked Chaudhary Brahm Prakash when he was the Chief Minister of Delhi and close to then PM Mr Nehru about raising Ahir Regiment, (I and Wing Commander Suresh Chaudhary son of Chaudhary Brahm Prakash's son were present) Chaudhary Brahm Prakash remained silent but did mention that some

Minister in the Mr Nehru's Government had some reservation about the Ahir Regiment. Maj Gen S D S Yadava who had been very passionate about Ahir Regiment where he talks about in his book FOLLOWERS OF LORD KRISHNA.

Mr Chanderjit Yadav was one of the Young Turk who helped Mrs Indira Gandhi against the all-powerful Syndicate was unsuccessful in persuading the then Government for an Ahir Regiment.

There were 2 very powerful Ahir leaders in UP and Bihar, they were Chief Minister of their state, later they were Cabinet Ministers with Govt Of India holding important ministries. It is unfortunate that these Leaders with their standing with the Government and influence were unable to find favourable response from the government then for Ahir Regiment

My father who was with the Kumaon Regiment Centre in the thirties as Jamadar Adjutant, at the centre then at Agra, mentioned many years later that the Ahirs of the region did not want the Kumaon Regiment Centre to move from Agra to Ranikhet which did not go down well with senior Cabinet Ministers, not that this had anything to do with the Ahir Regiment. But ?

After having said above, yeh sahi moka hai, (MODI HAI THO MUMKIN HAI). I am also the firm belief that Our PM would be aware of the dedication and bravery of the Ahir in the every theatre of war. I am sure in heart of heart, he would be convinced that the demand for Ahir Regiment is GENUINE. It is up to our Ahir Leaders approach him. (It's our only chance)

For our honourable ministers:

Mr Bhupender Singh and Mr Rao Intermit Singh.

(Our Ahir Leaders from UP and Bihar is a big disappointment.)

Dedicated to

To My Parents

Captain Puran Singh

Sardar Bahadur, OBI

&

Shrimati Bhagwan Kaur

They thrived on the ambition

To provide all those they loved

With comfort and care

That reached out far beyond

Even their own dreams

OUR PRAYER

My wife and I were under severe stress after learning about the heinous and brutal killings of Captain Saurabh Kalia, Squadron Leader Ajay Ahuja who was shot after he had ejected from his MiG-21, and Flt. Lt. Nachiketa who had been taken as prisoner and released after few days. Our son, then Sqn. Ldr. Monish was also flying into the Kargil area and was also the subject of our stress and worry.

From May to July 1999, we spent at least an hour in the temple praying for the safety of our son and all those participating in the Kargil conflict.

In the end, we were very happy and proud that our son was the one who had fired the Laser Guided Bomb (LGB) on Tiger Hill successfully, which ended the war.

Contents

Foreword

Having spent a lifetime on a particular profession leaves an indelible imprint on the mind of an individual, more so when life story has been remarkable. So is the story of Air Commodore V S Yadav, an accomplished aviator. I served under him while posted as the Senior Medical Officer of Air Force Station, Bombay, and frankly speaking I did not know his family's martial background, nor his remarkable accomplishments during his service career. He rightly regales in the fact of his forefathers having contributed to the first and the Second World War, and subsequently in the Kargil Battle. So, it is a story of velour and commitment clearly visible in the narrative.

His childhood, and student career was full of achievements, he was good at sports, hockey, football, and athletics, and was star sportsman of his school. In the service as well, he was sought after person in sports and athletics. His service career of course, is full of marvel, and achievements. His determination to join the armed forces is quite evident from the fact that he joined as a recruit with Kumaon Regiment and then worked towards getting a commission with the Air Force. He did not flinched an eyelid to join as a recruit, despite being educationally highly qualified.

Remembering centuries of history without records is challenging. I am not sure whether Air Commodore Yadav had a written record of his family's background, but whatever may be, the fact is he has penned a saga of proud legacy in a very interesting manner. Recalling events centuries before, and that too, in an authentic manner shows the power of narrative he displays. When the present and the past merge together pebbles in a stream make music. And that is exactly what the book displays.

Not only his family background but also his service career makes one feel drawn to a sense of awe and wonder. In his service career he achieved a lot. Not many people have the ability to recall events with so much clarity, and pen these down in an interesting fashion. It is not easy to fly carrying VIPs on board and escape scatheless. There are many ifs and buts in such a kind of service, and he has beautifully described these in the book.

His schooling and his focused agenda to join the armed forces were remarkable, as narrated in the book. He was so deeply drawn to join the armed forces that repeated failure in the UPSC examination or not being selected at the Selection Board did not deter him, and he wisely decided and joined the Kumaon Regiment as a recruit. But the fire to obtain an officers' grade burned in his heart continuously. And finally, he succeeded in getting selected for the direct entry for the Air Force Flying Branch. This shows not only a focused approach but also grit and determination.

This book will be of immense relevance to the Air Force. Surely the Air Force will find it worthwhile to have it in their chain of libraries.

With Best Wishes,

Laljee Verma
(Air Mshl L K Verma, AVSM, Retired)

Preface

Warriors are not born but forged through generations of sacrifice, courage, and resilience. This book is a tribute to three generations of my family who have dedicated their lives to defending the nation, facing near-fatal situations on the battlefield or in the skies. From Capt. Hari Singh, Capt. Puran Singh in the World War I to the valiant efforts of Gp. Capt. Monish Yadav in Kargil, our journey has been one of unwavering service, sacrifice, and survival.

One fateful day, in the skies over London, survival took on a new meaning for me. Seconds stood between life and death, and my entire life flashed before me in those moments. I was a young co-pilot aboard an Indian Air Force Super Constellation aircraft approaching RAF Northolt in London. A routine descent turned into a near-tragedy when a miscalculated approach put us on a collision course with a 637 feet hill.

"Victor Uniform Quebec Lima Delta (VUQLD), this is Northolt Radar. I have lost you on my screen. Request your height."

"500 feet, Sir," replied, VLD.

"VUQLD, if you read me, hill straight ahead 637 feet two miles – climb immediately to 1,500 feet, turn left!"

The Capt. continued the descent, oblivious to the looming danger. It took me 20 excruciating seconds to realise the gravity of the situation. We were lower than the hill – seconds away from disaster. Without hesitation, I yelled for full take-off power, yanked the controls, and pulled up harshly, praying we would make it in time.

Now at 400 feet, with mere seconds to impact, my mind was racing –

not with fear, but with a lifetime of memories. My wife, just two years into our marriage, our one-year-old son, my mother's prayers, the burning pain of childhood failures, my days at Sanawar, the discipline of military life, and the dream of flying – all flashed before my eyes. I braced for the impact.

And then – silence!

We had cleared the hill. Barely!

As we levelled off at 1,500 feet, another shock awaited us – a near-collision with a Columbia Airways Boeing 727 approaching Heathrow. The pilot later said that in 30 years of flying, he had never heard another aircraft so close in the air. It was a miracle that two catastrophes were averted in mere seconds.

We owed our lives to the sharp instincts of Flying Officer M.J. Eaton, the Northolt Radar Controller, who made the fateful call to climb turn left – a decision that saved us from the hill and avoided a mid-air disaster over Heathrow.

News of the near-miss made headlines on BBC and Indian news channels. At home, my family was still mourning the passing of my mother just three months earlier. When they heard what had happened, shock turned into gratitude – another tragedy had been narrowly avoided.

My Squadron mates' wives rushed to my wife, "Congratulations, Renu! Vijai has had a second life!" But as she processed the news, she realised what could have been – a widow at 21, a child without a father. The thought was chilling. For hours, she sat in stunned silence, waiting for me to return, knowing how close she had come to losing everything.

That day in the skies over London changed me for ever. It made me value life, purpose, and the responsibilities of wearing the uniform.

But this book is not just about me – it is about a family forged in service. It is about my father, uncles, cousins, and those who came before us, dedicating their lives to serving the nation. It is about battlefields, trenches, skies, and the unseen sacrifices that military families make and the tensions they endure.

It is about honour, duty, and resilience.

This is the story of a *Haryanvi chhora* born in the dusty village of Sadat Nagar (Nayagaon), Rewari, with no roads, no transportation, and limited opportunities – who defied the odds to take flight. This journey began in war-torn trenches and soared into the skies.

As I sit down to pen these words, I realise that the journey has always been more beautiful than the destination.

Air Commodore Vijai Singh Yadav (V)

Prologue

I come from a simple Haryanvi family where serving the nation was a way of life. My father fought in World War I, and many others in our family also wore the uniform with pride. Growing up in such an atmosphere of discipline and sacrifice, I too was inspired to follow that path. From being a village boy, a Haryanvi chhora, I rose to wear the blue uniform of the Indian Air Force - something that once seemed far beyond my reach.

This book is not just about my journey, but about the spirit of countless men and women who chose service above self.

Their courage, sacrifice, and determination remain a legacy for all of us to carry forward.

Many facets of my journey has helped in shaping my character and personality. My mental capacity to face failures as a blessing in disguise and my successes as an identification to be a good leader.

Acknowledgements

It was Air Officer Commanding-in-Chief, Central Air Command, Air Marshal Ripu Sahni who first suggested I write my memoirs after witnessing the presentation of President's Colours to my Squadron. After retirement, I did make an attempt but found it difficult and so I gave up. Years later, at the Air Officer's lunch, Air Marshal Sahni asked inquired if I had written my memoirs and suggested again that I take it up.

Recently during the book club meeting at the Venu Eye Institute, of which I am a member, Mr. Tarun Basu, a well-known editor and journalist wanted to know about my experiences with Indian Air Force.

Mr Basu arranged a meeting with Mr. Rajan Arya of Pentagon Press LLP advised me to start writing.

I am grateful to Mr. Tarun Basu for his motivation and guidance. I would like to thank my editor, who helped me with a lot of re-writing and editing. He prefers to remain anonymous.

I am also grateful to my family members who have helped wherever needed. My two nephews, Major Ashok and Lt. Gen. Karan, my son, Gp. Capt. Monish, and my granddaughter, Shreya. My wife helps me with her critical views.

Air Commodore Vijai Singh Yadav (V)

Note to Readers...

Dear Reader,

This is the story of a boy born in a dusty, sleepy, and underdeveloped village in the backwards regions of Haryana. A boy who belonged to a large semi-joint family, where he was often seen as underdeveloped, even invisible. That boy ... was me.

My early education was a mix of languages – primary school in Urdu, middle school in Hindi, and high school in English. The result? I wasn't truly fluent in any of them. English, especially, remained a struggle. And yet, somehow – perhaps through some unknown external grace – I found the strength to write.

In the beginning, I was even confused about something as basic as the difference between a Preface, a Prologue, and an Author's Note. I searched for books by great authors, biographies of renowned personalities, hoping to find guidance. What I discovered was that most of them didn't rely on introductions – their names were enough.

In my case, I have no such claim to fame. I'm neither a celebrated author nor a public figure. I'm just someone who felt compelled to share his story – in the hope that parts of it might resonate with you.

If the Preface is where challenges are revealed, and the Prologue is where the character is shaped – then let this Note to Readers be my honest attempt to connect with you, heart to heart.

Thank you for picking up this book. I hope it leaves behind more than just words – I hope it leaves behind a feeling.

Warmly,

Vijai Yadav

Chapter One

A Legacy of Service

ANCESTORS

The Yadav dynasty had been greatly weakened by fratricidal wars. Finally, in the 14th century, Sultan Alauddin Khilji of the Delhi Sultanate decided to annex the Yadav kingdom. He sent his army under General Malik Kafur who comprehensively defeated the Yadavs. The assault was ruthless but many Ahir (Yadav) families escaped to various parts of the country. It is believed that our ancestors moved to the north-western part of India.

As the story goes, around the 15th century, the family spiritual head advised that their current location was not ideal for final settlement and told the family to prepare and move towards the south-east. He (addressed as Gusain) is the father figure of the family; he maintains the family financial and land holding records, is the final arbitrator, and his decisions are never disputed. Our family then consisted of two brothers, namely, Bhairu Singh and the younger, Kishan Lal with their followers, and the Guru. They halted at a place which is now known as Kanina (in present-day Mahendergarh district of Haryana). While they were settling there, the wife of the younger brother sent a message to her elder brother-in-law if he could shift a little further so that the movement of ladies was not inhibited because of the strict *purdah* system. He did not take this kindly as women in those days were not supposed to be heard or seen. Bhairu Singh, in anger, moved with his followers to present-day Bhairod in Rajasthan and sent word to his sister-in-law in sarcastic way if his new location was OK. According to ancestral lore, it was thus that Kishan Lal and his followers established Kanina village (named after him). Similarly, Bhairod was established by Bhairu Singh and his followers. (It's only the family belief, not historical researched.)

We have been able to trace our ancestors to 11 generations from the 17th to the 21st century. As the founder of our clan was Kishan Lal of Kanina, we acquired the *gotra* (sub caste) Kaninwal. (Our family tree is attached, starting with Chaudhary Harsevak down to Aryaman, my eldest brother's great grandson.)

The authenticity of the genealogy was researched by my father and we were able to confirm from Garhmuktheshwar (the holy site where our family's last rites are performed and ashes immersed), where the family *pandas* (hereditary keepers of clan records) keep the *bahi* (ledger) of the family.

The First World War and The Beginning of our Martial Tradition

I want to write about the First World War (WW I) where my *Tauji* (uncle) and my father were part of the 1.4 million soldiers who participated in it. For our family, it was a beginning that led to a new chapter.

The 1.4 million Indian soldiers who participated in WW I from 1914 to 1918 left an indelible stamp on every theatre of the Great War. I am proud to mention that 11 Victoria Crosses (VCs), the highest gallantry award of the British Commonwealth, were awarded to Indian Soldiers. It is a matter of pride to mention that my *Tauji* (uncle) and my father were part of those Indian Soldiers who displayed the highest courage, discipline, devotion and staked their lives for honour and duty.

Rao Devi Sahay, *zamindar* (landlord) of village Gawadi, Tehsil Nahar, married off his daughter, Maryam Kaur to Ch. Man Singh, one of the four sons of Ch. Anup Singh (my great grandfather), landlord of village Kanina. He had one request – that the newlyweds move in with him permanently. Ch. Anup Singh was a little hesitant as Rao Devi Sahay had a son who, as per tradition, would rightfully inherit his property. However, Rao Devi

Sahay assured that his property will be shared equally by his son and daughter – those days a man's word had more worth than an agreement in any court! He explained that he wished his daughter and son-in-law would assist him to establish a new village at the behest of the Nawab of Dujana (his friend and a dice partner). He hoped thus to tackle the problems he was having with the population of Nahar.

After the new village was established, Rao Devi Sahay asked his son and son-in-law to divide his property equally as his health was deteriorating. His son-in-law declined the offer as he felt there was perfect understanding between him and his brother-in-law. However, fate intervened. Rao Devi Sahay, his son, Rao Sheotaj Singh and son-in-law Ch. Man Singh expired within a few months of each other. Ch. Man Singh's widow was requested to return to her village of Kanina with her children. As was customary, daughters did not have the right to inheritance. Thus, Ch. Man Singh's widow, Maryam Kaur, felt let down that her father's word had not been honoured. However, she did not contest and requested her eldest son, Ch. Hari Singh (later Capt. Hari Singh), then still a teenager, to meet his three uncles (Ch. Man Singh's brothers) at Kanina and apprise them of the circumstances. The uncles politely told the boy that the property had already been distributed and no change was possible. A chastened Hari Singh returned with the responsibility to take care of his mother, two brothers and a sister. After taking stock of the situation and their strained circumstances, he decided that younger brother, Ch. Puran Singh (later Capt. Puran Singh) would continue to go to school, his elder brother, Ch. Sadhu Singh and sister Prem Kaur would assist their mother, and he would join the army to support the family.

A massive recruitment drive was on in India in those days to recruit men to serve in the army in the First World War. He knew of the high rate of casualties in the European theatre but his strained circumstances left him with no choice as he was the sole support of his family. His youngest brother, Ch. Puran Singh, would follow in his footsteps later.

Though the family tried to cope bravely with their dire financial situation, it proved too much for the mother, Maryam Kaur, and she eventually suffered a paralytic attack. (What my sister tells me is that more than the loss of property, my grandmother was hit by the shift in loyalty and respect.)

My father, Ch. Puran Singh, being the youngest child, had been pampered but retained the pride of the son of a *zamindar*. He adjusted admirably to the trying circumstances. He moved to Rewari for high school and did well there, particularly in sports, but noticed that the family was still struggling as the lone working brother's earnings were not sufficient. He too decided to join the army, though without the knowledge of his brother and mother.

Both my uncle (*Tauji*) and my father rendered exemplary service with dedication, devotion to duty and loyalty and were awarded the coveted Order of British India (OBI) which carried the title 'Sardar Bahadur'. My *Tauji*, who retired after the Second World War, and my father, who retired just after Independence, were awarded land, as was the practice in the days of the British Raj. My *Tauji* was allotted land in Lahore district (now in Pakistan), but in 1946 was able to get the land grant transferred to Rewari district. Unfortunately, my father, who was also allotted a land grant in what was to become West Pakistan, could not manage a similar transfer. He could not 'navigate' past the *babus*, and refused to stand the harassment. He placed his dignity and honour above being allotted few hundred *bighas* of land.

Blessing in Disguise

The crisis that arose after the demise of their father and thus losing their property overnight, compelled my *Tauji* (uncle) and my father to join the army to support the family. In reality, this proved to be a blessing in disguise while they served in the country and abroad, they realised the importance of education and decided to pool their resources to impart the best education available in the country to their children. My *Tauji* put his son in the Prince of Wales RIMC (now Rashtriya Indian Military College), Dehradun and my father enrolled his two elder sons in KG High School, Ajmer, and his two younger sons in Lawrence School, Sanawar. They all went on to join the defence services as officers, then considered to be most sought after, honourable and prestigious calling – the profession of arms.

Thus, began my family's martial tradition in the Modern Era.

The Centenary Year 2014 World War One (WW1)

The British Government decided to celebrate the centenary year in honour of the Indian troops who participated in the world war one (WW1) and in particularly the Victoria Cross Awardees.

I personally feel gratified to the British Government on behalf of my *Tauji* Captain Hari Singh and my father Captain Puran Singh who were part of the Indian Troops actively participated in the Great War (WW1)

I am therefore taking the opportunity to convey to our future generations, that it was a great gesture by then British Prime Minister to honour in memory of the Indian troops, decided to celebrate the centenary year of the WW1. My write up then becomes the record for all our future generation, and a small brief about the celebration for their benefit.

The then Prime Minister Mr David Camron and his government took massive publicity exercise that the year 2014 is the centenary year of the First World War (WW1) and expressed to be a truly national moment, particularly to honour the Indian troops participated in the war. The British High Commissioner to India Sir James Beven held a reception to honour and recognise the Indian troops at the United Services Institute (USI) when Lt Gen P K Singh was its Director. It was heartening and a moving event to watch the Indian troops fighting during the war and their each and every activities. It was very thoughtful gesture of the British High Commissioner to obtain all details from the war museum and the British Archives of the Indian troops.

The British Defence Secretary Mr Michael Fallen also held a reception and announced that the British is building a memorial at six (6) Regimental Centres to honour the Indian Victoria Cross winners. The Indian Defence Minister who was present at the reception conveyed his gratitude of this great gesture by the British government, he also informed that the Indian Government under PM Narender Bhai Modi is building a massive War Memorial at India Gate to honour the brave Indian troops who fought in every war all over the world and in every theatre.

It is a great feeling by each and every citizen of our country to feel proud of our troops who laid their life for a cause and their country. The families from those who took part in the war finds an opportunity to pay their obeisance at the war museum.

This chapter therefore is for our family and future generations to feel proud of Captain Hari Singh and Captain Puran Singh.

Highest Gallantry Awards for Valour

The Victoria Cross (VC) and the Param Vir Chakra (PVC) were introduced in recognition for those who displayed extra ordinary courage and bravery in the face of enemy. My attention was drawn to the inscription on the Victoria Cross as **FOR Valour** therefore my curiosity to learn about the VC its origin, its design and their historical back ground, and also to know about **Param Vir Chakra** (PVC).

Victoria Cross (VC)

It was felt during the Crimean War, distinct, exemplary and display of extra ordinary courage and bravery in the face of enemy should be suitably awarded for their recognition, the Victoria Cross (VC) as the highest gallantry award was introduced on 29th January 1856.

The bronze from which all Victoria Cross are made by the Central Ordinance in Donnington, the metal is cut from the cannon captured from the Russian at SEBASTOPOL during the Crimean war. The medal was designed by the London Jewellers & Co. and For Valour is inscribed. The word Valour is derived from Latin **Valorem** meaning strength, moral worth added as courage, but the British described Valour as Honour, Dignified Bravery and men of steel.

Param Vir Chakra (PVC)

The Param Vir Chakra (PVC) was instituted by the President of India Dr Rajender Prasad on 26 January 1950 on Republic Day with retrospective effect from 15 August 1947, for the wheel of the ultimate brave. The award is for the most Conspicuous Bravery in the face of enemy.

The Medal is cast in bronze, in the centre on a raised circle is the state emblem surrounded by for replica of Indian Vajra flanked by the sword of Shivaji Maharaj, with 32 MM purple ribbon.

The Param Vir Chakra (PVC) was designed by Mrs Savitri Khanolkar, (a Swiss Indian designer) she drew inspiration from Sage DADHICHI a Vedic Rishi who made the ultimate sacrifice by giving up his body so that the Gods could make a deadly weapon called VAJRA or THUNDERBOLT from his spine.

Mrs Savitri Khanolkar is originally Swiss born as Eve Yuonne Mayday De Maros.

There have been 21 Indian Defence personnel Param Vir Chakra Awardees, 21 Islands in the Andaman & Nicobar Islands have been named after each of these awardees. This gesture and great honour given to them by the Modi Gornment.

Next For Valour the Indian Soldier.

Three Generations in Wars

It is my proud privilege to mention that our family (Kaninwal) were active participants in all the wars fought by the Indian Defence Services from the First World War (1914-18) to the 1999 Kargil War. This is a brief account of the participation of our three generations.

My *Tauji* (Uncle), Captain Hari Singh, Sardar Bahadur, OBI ORDER OF BRITISH INDIA (SBOBI)

Hari Singh was the eldest of the siblings of my father's generation. He joined the army during the First World War). He had an excellent record of dedication and hard work, for which he was awarded the Sardar Bahadur Order of British India (OBI). He served as an Instructor in the Kitchener Military College in Peshawar; attended the coronation of King George VI in 1937, retired in 1946 and settled initially in our ancestral village, Sadat Nagar, before shifting to Rewari after he was allotted land there. In July 1947, our village was attacked by about 100 Muslim soldiers. While there were no casualties, all weapons – rifles, swords, daggers – were confiscated. Hearing about the presence of a decorated veteran in the village (my *Tauji*), the Muslim officer leading the attackers went to meet him. He saw a photograph of my cousin, Captain (later Colonel) Ram Singh.

Colonel Ram Singh, son of my *tauji* Captain Hari Singh, took pre mature retirement, and join politics became minister in PV Narasimha Rao Government. When told that he was Captain Hari Singh's son he said that Ram Singh was his batch mate in the Academy. The officer had a cup of tea and returned all the confiscated weapons.

My Father, Captain Puran Singh, Sardar Bahadur, OBI (SB OBI)

My father joined the army as a boy at the fag end of the First World War in 1918. He was an active participant during WW II in the Burma front. For his hard work, dedication, and loyalty, he was Mentioned in Despatches (a gallantry award) and awarded the Sardar Bahadur Order of British India (OBI) and land. Though he was selected for an officer's commission in 1938/39, his unit Second-in-Command (2/IC) requested him to turn down the offer as he wanted him to be his Subedar Major during his command of 2/19 Hyderabad, later 2 Kumaon). The Second World War was looming over the horizon. My father accepted the suggestion.

Around the end of WW II, when Indian Army units were sent to restore peace in the former European colonies that had been taken over by the Japanese, my father's unit was deployed in one of the Dutch East Indies colonies. There were Dutch troops serving alongside my father's battalion. An order was issued that the Dutch troops would not salute or pay compliments to the Indian JCO (Junior Commissioned Officers) which did not go down well with the Indian troops, who planned a protest. This was a dangerous situation during war. My father with help of his CO saved the situation.

Captain Puran Singh was adjudged the best turned-out soldier of the Indian Army. He was selected to attend the coronation of King George VI; however, his elder brother, Capt. Hari Singh, then the Subedar Major of the battalion, attended. My father was obsessed with his military uniform. Though they were issued free, he would still buy new ones the moment he thought that the 'newness' had faded. He retired in 1948 after serving in the Army for four decades.

Major General Shiv Dayal Singh Yadava

Maj. Gen. S.D.S. Yadava, my eldest brother, was commissioned in the Indian Army in 1946 when he was less than 19 years old and the Second World War had just ended. He joined 2/3 Gurkhas as a young subaltern. He was a hard core disciplinarian. He spared neither himself, nor his family and would do things only the right way. He was truly a father figure to us siblings. He had a glorious and satisfying career. An upright and sincere officer, promoted to Brigadier when only 40 years old, he took command of 41 Mountain Brigade at Ahlelal in Himachal from where he moved the Brigade to Lucknow. During his leave with us at Pune in early 1971, the Army Chief, General (later Field Marshal) Manekshaw cut short his leave and asked him to take command of 61 Mountain Brigade in the North East Sector, bordering East Pakistan (now Bangladesh).

During the run up to the 1971 War, the Corps Commander ordered 61 Mountain Brigade to attack the Pakistan border outpost at Dhalai on 31 October 1971. Dhalai was manned by a full battalion-sized force that could cause heavy casualties. There *were* very heavy casualties. The Commanding Officer of 7 Raj. Rif., Lt. Col. Devsan was seriously wounded, also the Brigade Commander, Brig. S.D.S. Yadava. He was too gravely wounded. He was lucky to be evacuated time which saved his life and his right leg. The sad part is that many valuable lives were lost. It was learnt that the Brigadier who took over from Brig. Yadava was awarded for the Dhalai action.

Lt. Col. Ratan Singh Yadav

Lt. Col. Ratan Singh, my elder brother, was commissioned in 1948. While undergoing the higher command course at Infantry School, Mhow, he was asked to cut short his course to train the Bangladeshi Mukti Bahini. He was thereafter fully involved with them in their operations and achieved favourable results against the Pakistan Army. In recognition of his services, he was Mentioned-in Despatches. He took premature retirement in 1984.

Lt. Col. Aman Singh Yadav

My younger brother, Lt. Col. Aman Singh Yadav was commissioned in 1961. He was serving as an Instructor at Infantry School, Mhow in 1971 when he was ordered to join his battalion at the front. He retired in 1991.

Lt. Gen. Karan Singh Yadava

Lt. Gen. Karan Singh Yadava, son of my eldest brother, Maj. Gen. S.D.S. Yadava, was commissioned in 1971. As a young Subaltern, he served with his battalion on the Chinese border at Hyuliang/Walong. He held an important operational appointment in J&K during the Kargil War. He retired in 2010 as DG Assam Rifles. (His decorate PVSM, AVSM, SM, VSM.)

Major Ashok Singh Yadav

Major Ashok Singh Yadav, my sister's son, was also commissioned in 1971. As a young subaltern, he was with 7 Para in the Western Sector. He took premature retirement in 1993. He felt the need to establish good schools to provide quality education in backward southern Haryana so that local children could compete with those from more developed urban areas. His efforts have borne fruit. He is now providing free education (including boarding, lodging, uniforms, books, etc.) to children of martyred defence personnel. He also donates funds to NGOs run by defence officers if he feels they are doing genuine charity work.

Group Captain Monish Yadav

Group Captain Monish Yadav, my elder son, was commissioned in the Indian Air Force in 1991 in the fighter stream. He was an active participant in the Kargil War. The task to fire the Laser Guided Bomb (LGB) at the Pakistani intruders was given to his Squadron, which was flying the Mirage 2000. He was the only one who successfully fired the LGB, which went a long way in ending the conflict. Monish took premature retirement in 2012. He was also the part of Indian Air Force aerobatic team, Surya Kiran.

Air Commodore Vijai Singh Yadav (the author)

Commissioned in 1961 in the Indian Air Force, I was with the Maritime Squadron of the Indian Air Force during the 1971 War. Our Squadron was tasked with reconnaissance and patrolling of Karachi harbour round the clock, monitoring each shipping movement there. We guided the rescue operation when *INS Khukri* was sunk. I retired in 1993, also participates in 1962 and 1965.

Facilitation by the Government of Punjab

The Chief Minister of Punjab Mr Pratap Singh Kairon requested all veterans to come to Chandigarh who contributed more than 2 sons and participated in the war against China in 1962. My father was given special honour for giving all his 4 sons to the Armed Forces and all participated in war against China.

We all brothers shared are experiences with father about the war with China, we all agreed that the main reason of defeat.

One, Incompetent Leadership at the Military Level.

Two, The political level leadership as described by experts as Irresolute, weak, uncertain, hesitant, indecisive resulted in poor strategic and tactical planning. The Army was pushed, unprepared, unequipped and untimely.

The Indian Soldier who are considered to be the best fighters in the world faced such humiliation and their pride staked.

Field Marshal Sir Claude John Eyre Auchinleck GCB GCIE CSI DSO OBE, supposed to have said

> *"For many years I have wished that the story of the Indian Army in the 2nd World War (WW2) might be written so that for the people of his country could learn what they owe to those Indian soldiers who fought for them against the Germans, Japanese and Italians, without the aid of the Indian Soldiers the war could NOT have been won".*

Honour by the Chief of Army Staff

Gen Manekshaw (later Field Marshal) COAS visited my eldest brother in the Army Hospital Delhi Cantt where he was admitted after he was seriously wounded in the battle of Dhalai, war with Pakistan in1971.

The Army Chief facilitated my father Capt. Puran Singh for contributed all his 4 sons and two grandsons to the Armed Forces and fully participated in the war with Pakistan in 1971. (Captain Sahab I am very happy to meet you, Army Chief)

Mrs Indira Gandhi through a letter addressed to Gen Manekshaw complemented of his brilliant leadership and complete cooperation of the 3 services which lead to the victory over Pakistan. The Shimla Agreement was a blunder.

The Three Generations and the Regiments/Squadrons they Served

Chapter Two

Early Years and Education

CHILDHOOD AS *DHAULL*

I was seventh from the bottom among 17 boys and 11 girls in a semi joint family of six brothers and cousins. The age difference between the eldest and the youngest was more than 20 years. The parents rarely concentrated on bringing up the children; it was the elder siblings who looked after the younger kids and maintained discipline. The eldest sibling of each family was regarded as the father figure with equal respect and therefore there was never an occasion of being thrashed or raising of voices. Though all the children were normal and growing well, it was noticed that I was far too meek, timid, docile, quiet, shy, and uncomfortable among elders. If any of the parents or elder siblings called to say something nice about me or give me some minor job, I would invariably tremble in their presence. With this nature, I was branded among the family as a *Dhaull.*

The term '*dhaull*' comes from the *jowar* or sorghum plant. When the plant becomes hollow or useless, the middle of its leaves turns white – in this state it is called *dhaull.*

My initial schooling was in the only primary school in the village. On one occasion when the teacher called me, I started to tremble. He asked me as to why I was trembling (*tum kamp kau rahe ho*) and decreed that from the next day, I would lead the reciting of the tables. Next day, he told my father that *Bije* (as I was known then) trembled when called to lead the recitation of multiplication tables despite being good at them. My father replied that *Bije dil ka thoda kamjor hai.*

On the other hand, when among friends, my character was totally different. In the company of friends I was at ease – very talkative, comfortable, and feeling important. Therefore, I would look for every opportunity to be with friends rather than with the family.

I was fond of climbing trees and buildings. I would demonstrate to my friends how to jump from one branch to another. Once while showing my friends how to climb a building, I fell on my left knee on a very sharp stone. The result was a deep cut and profuse bleeding. In an effort to stop the bleeding, I stuffed mud in a cloth, and used it as a dressing. Afraid of the scolding that would surely follow my recklessness; I kept quiet till my mother noticed the makeshift bandage. Thereupon, a paste of atta and *haldi* (turmeric) with the hair of old ladies was promptly applied (the local remedy for all kinds of wounds). It did help and prevented the wound from becoming septic though it left a permanent scar which became my identification mark!

I was an active participant with my friends in village functions whereas my cousins rarely took part. During *Teej* festivities, it was *fora* (long jump); in pre-Diwali it was *hooll* (rural hockey). In both, I was found to be far above average. Pre-Holi all the peasants, labourers, villagers would get together for folk songs and humorous plays which we children were not permitted to attend. Since I knew my friends would be there, I would always slip out and join them.

This side of my personality was not known to the family; therefore I remained a *dhaull* for them. I was never ridiculed or humiliated at being called a *dhaull* but probably must have felt stifled which may have made me stubborn and difficult towards my mother. I remember returning from school during lunch break and asking mother from outside the house "*Ma, roti tayyar sai?*" She would reply, "*Ha bhai, tawa pe sai*" (Ma is my lunch ready... Yes it is on the *tawa*). Knowing that it would take a little more time for lunch to be actually served, I would then run back to the school with my mother running after me calling out that lunch was ready; I did not want to lose even a minute with my friends. After that, mother always kept the lunch ready, but also learnt that I would take anything up to almost 10 minutes to clean the wooden slate and then daubing it with *Multani mitti* (to be used the next day). So even if lunch was not ready, mother would always say it was as she would get those 10 minutes to serve it.

Mother also learnt the extent of my fondness for my friends. Once she noticed that I was limping. On questioning I told her that while returning from school my feet had been exposed to the hot sand (I had taken off my Juties). She asked me where my *jutis* (shoes) were. In my bag, I replied, because my friends, Srichand and Birbal, were bare foot. Off, she went complaining to my father: "Oh my God, what to do with this child? He will do everything for others but nothing for himself – to the extent that he will hurt himself to help others. I am really worried about him." Father then mentioned that Seekhsan, our family *mochi* (cobbler), had come to tell father that *Bije dau chhora le kar aaya tho ke, oon ke liye juti banau* (*Bije* brought two boys to make shoes for them). In my innocence I thought that the *mochi* was supposed to make *jutis* for everyone, just as he used to make for our family.

Another peculiar habit I had was that if I was scolded or punished for something I had not done, I would never explain or contest. On one occasion, ink had spilt and my elder brother thought I had done it. Initially I kept quiet, but when he said I would not be punished if I told the truth, I maintained that I was not responsible. My brother was not convinced and so I started crying; he then hugged me. (How difficult it is to explain that **Truth to be True.**) I always shielded my loneliness, just as I did my feelings.

Most of the houses in the village were built with mud; our *haveli* was big enough to house six families. Each family had a room on the first floor called *chaubara*. Normally this room was built for the newly married. Apart from being used as a bedroom, it also has an outlet for water so that the new brides could bathe there. It has been customary in our family for the ladies to be assisted or bathed by the domestic help. I remember one such occasion (I must have been around five years old or less) when my sister-in-law was being bathed. I happened to be around and wanted to know why the room was closed. When I tried to enter, the help banged the door shut, with the result that the tip of my little finger got cut.

An interesting insight: In those days, villages in our area had a common well-centrally located. There was a large tank which was filled in mornings in winter and in the evenings in summer for the men to bathe and also wash their cattle. (We had our own private well.) The village women, on the other hand, bathed secluded on the roof of their mud houses – which is why no one was allowed to ride a camel through the village!

After primary school, I was sent to the high school at Rewari.

"I was unique mix of Meekness and Enthusiasm out of place everywhere at home nowhere."

High School Years (Rewari and Sanawar)

Rewari

After clearing primary school (class IV) I was sent to the nearest town, Rewari, for further education. I was admitted in Class V of the Rao Bahadur Balbir Singh High School there. It was the only good high school in the vicinity and my *Tauji*, Capt. Hari Singh, lived adjacent to it.

I was scared and nervous when I learnt that I was being sent to Rewari. It was natural that I was distressed because I was to be uprooted from where I felt comfortable and found happiness with my mother and friends. Even though I was troublesome to my mother and made unreasonable demands and throwing tantrums now and then, she was never annoyed or irritated. Similarly, I was happy with my friends and feeling important. I was too meek and afraid to voice my feelings. It was my mother and my friends in whom I found solace and now I was to be away from them.

I was lucky to get a room in the school hostel which overlooked *Tauji's* house. Initially, I felt so lonely that I would often run over to *Tauji's* house where my *Taiji* (elder aunt) would pamper me with food and ask if I had any problems. It made me feel a bit better but I still missed my mother and friends.

Although *Taiji* was some help, I was unable to adjust to my new surroundings and remained aloof. I just couldn't make friends and that started affecting my studies. One weekend I was so depressed that I caught a train for home. Even before entering the house, I called out "*Maa, dahi se?*" (Mother, is there curd?). "*Na Bhai, dophar mai dhahi nahi rakhte*", (No, we don't keep curd in the afternoon.) (In those days only as much curd as was required in the mornings by the family was made, the remainder was churned into butter. Besides, curd or butter milk is not consumed in the afternoons or evenings.) In fit of stubbornness, without even entering the house, I caught the next train back to Rewari. Mother ran out to pacify me but I believe I did not even look back! Now, when I look back at my crass behaviour, I curse myself.

Thereafter, on every weekend, a *dahi katori* (bowl of curd) was always kept for me. Subsequently, once I had adjusted in Rewari, my trips home lessened. On one occasion, going home after a long break, I noticed our dog, Basu, sprinting away. It was actually to tell mother that I had come. She and the dog came running out and the first thing she said was, "*Bhai dahi se*". I had even forgotten by then that I had ever asked for curd. I remember feeling so bad; my eyes moistened and I hugged her for the first time.

My trips home from Rewari were by train to Kosli railway station which is about three-four kilometres from our village. Everyone bound for the village walked. On one occasion, when I was going back to Rewari, my father accompanied me to the railway station. The station master, who knew my father, told him "*Bije ek bahut achha siddha aur baddo ki kadar karne wala bacha hai*". (Vijai is a good and simple kid who respects his elders). He (the station master) would tell me to collect my ticket from inside his office, but I would always stand in the queue like everyone else. I remember I always travelled second class on half fare (those days there were four categories of rail of travel: 1st class, 2nd, Inter and 3rd class; children below 12 were charged half the normal fare).

Sports at school were mainly hockey, tug-of-war, and *kabaddi;* in athletics, there were only short races, long jump, and shot put. Generally, evening hockey matches would be organised in the hostel grounds. I was always there watching the games. On one occasion, when they were short of a player, I was asked to join. Excited at the invitation, I found that with a proper hockey stick and a ball I had much better control. I realised I could move much faster with the ball than while playing *hule* (rural hockey) with improvised hockey sticks and a ball. Thereafter, I became part of the hostel team and came to the notice of the school sports teacher. I noticed him coaching the tug-of-war school team in the hostel grounds. He would tie a rope to a tree, sit on it and tell the team to 'tug' it! He would tell the team that they should not allow the rope to sag even half an inch for at least half an hour; if it did then the time would be extended by another half an hour! Our school tug-of-war team naturally became the best in the district! The sports teacher wanted to know how old I was. When I told him I was 11, he hugged me and told me to join the school sport teams. Suddenly, I was interacting with the top players of the school. Since I was the youngest, I was encouraged and pampered. This was a great motivation for me to shed my shyness and meekness and I started gaining self-confidence.

Man Singh was the star player of not only the school but of the entire district. He was the role model for all sports enthusiasts. I was lucky that he often guided and made me improve. I later learnt that he had been selected to join Punjab Police out of turn for being an outstanding sportsman.

A year later I was promoted to class VI and my younger brother Aman joined the school in class V.

In 1950, two big events took place in our family. My sister gave birth to a boy on 10 January, and my elder sister-in-law gave birth to a boy on 24 September at Rewari. On both occasions I was asked to go to the village to break the welcome news to my parents who were waiting eagerly to hear it. It was a big celebration to have two grandsons in the same year.

Col. Bhagwan Singh of our village told my father that my younger brother and I be sent to the English medium school, Lawrence School at Sanawar near Kasauli, where his son was studying. My father discussed this with both his elder sons who were already army officers; they agreed in principle that good education was desirable.

They then discussed the financial aspect and whether Vijai (to the family I was still *Dhaull*) would benefit from it. My father told them about the primary teacher's positive remark and said he will go to Rewari to discuss with his brother, Capt. Hari Singh with whom I had been interacting with for the last two years and also check with the teachers there.

The immediate response of my *Tauji*, who always addressed me as *Bije* Bahadur, was that my younger brother and I should be sent to a good school for better prospects, and mentioned that his son had been admitted to RIMC, Dehradun. Both my elder brothers had gone to King George's School, Ajmer. *Tauji* told my father about when he had caught me with his .22 gun. Very scared, he did not scold me but made me fire at a small circle he made on the wall. My aim was good and I had hit the bull's eye. Asked who had taught me to fire so accurately, I replied "Nobody". I then mentioned that when *Tauji* Richhpal Singh had come to the village and shot a deer, his wife, *Taiji* Shanti, had invited me to have meal with them. There, I saw that *Tauji* was cleaning his rifle. I helped him to clean it and he taught me how to aim. My father was surprised but was happy. (Rao Richhpal Singh is the middle grandson of Rao Devi Sahay and maternal cousin of my father. He is basically a *shikari* (hunter) and lives with his younger son at Jhalawar Rajasthan; he comes to our village once a year.)

My father satisfied with his brother's response. He then met the school and sports teachers and they spoke highly about me. The sports teacher added that I had a great future and would be an outstanding sportsman.

Back in the village my mother said she had always known that I was not what the family thought. She said I was shy to speak or even show directly or indirectly what I truly was.

By then I had started to enjoy my stay at Rewari. My passion for sports and the guidance I was receiving changed my outlook and my behaviour. I started feeling happy, speaking a lot and no longer feeling uncomfortable among my seniors. This brought about a sea change in my personality – my drooping shoulders became erect and my gait confident – a spring in it. The news that my brother and I were being sent to an English school far away came as a bombshell. I retreated into my cocoon. However, my brother was excited.

Sanawar

Lawrence School Sanawar was founded more than 175 years ago by Sir Henry Lawrence in 1847. It was only meant for the children of British troops posted in India so that they could receive public school education as in England. My father was happy to learn that this was the only school patronised by royalty, the only school to receive the King's Colours and first co-education residential school. He later learnt that the renowned author, Rudyard Kipling, wrote in *KIM... "send Kim to Sanawar to make a man of him*". After Independence in 1947 the British student left and with help from the Government, the school continued as a public school with the British/European teaching staff continuing.

Admissions were easy as there were not many students then. We reached the school on 10 February 1951 after travelling by train to Kalka and then by road to the school. I was vomiting throughout the drive to the school.

We were allotted Himalaya House and father handed us over to the House Matron. She gave us our kit, including the school uniform, shoes, socks, underwear, and toiletries – almost everything we needed. We were then asked to change into the school dress put all the items we had brought into a box that was carried to the box room.

My father told the principal that he has some apprehension that his sons may be made to feel inferior just because their father was only a Subedar Major and Honorary Captain among children of General (later Field Marshal) Cariappa, the Maharajas of Patiala and Baroda, and some industrialists. The Principal assured him that once the children stepped into the school, they are treated as equals irrespective of who their parents are. After being told about the facilities in the school, my father described – it as a small close family living on a lush green hilltop with a single aim: to make their children (students) *Achhe aur nek insan.*

I was in a state of total withdrawal, confused, and depressed. I just followed the routine by observing what went on. My younger brother would help me once in a while; I noticed he was very comfortable and began speaking English that everybody was speaking within two days.

I can never forget the very first kit changing day. It was on the third day. I did not know that each boy was allotted a number, which was marked on each clothing item and allotted a slot in the store room. The house matron found that one kit was yet to be issued and exchanged. She called out my number of which I was not aware. I thought she was probably asking as to where our dirty clothes were so that they could be replaced with clean ones. She lost her patience and started shouting angrily. I got so scared that I was on the verge of wetting my pants! I just blurted out the two sentences I had learnt: that my name was Vijai Singh Yadav and my father's name was Captain Puran Singh. Suddenly she quietened down, smiled and hugged me. She called out to a boy to help me with the kit change. Thereafter, I became her favourite – she would often call me to sit with her and treated me like her grandson. Our house matron was the mother of the headmaster who was a bachelor.

Another ritual I noticed was the polishing of our shoes called brogues. After supper and before lights out, every one sat on their boxes with a candle, black polish, a little water in the cover of the polish can, a cloth and a shoe brush. The toes of the shoes were polished till they shone. After brushing the shoes, with a cloth-wrapped finger we applied polish on the toe, heated it with the candle and then burnished it with water. This process continued till one was satisfied with the shine.

I went through the daily routine like a dummy. We got up when the bugle was sounded and headed for PT/gymnastics. After that, we wore our school uniform and stood by our beds with everything folded and place correctly. Then the headmaster inspected – our hair cut, nails, ears, the uniform, and the shoes. After that we went for breakfast and then marched to the school building for classes. There was an hour's rest after lunch. This was followed by games and tea break. After the evening bath we returned to our class rooms for prep (homework). I learnt that the hockey season was to commence and teams were formed class and age-wise. To my excitement, within a week I was upgraded to the school colts' team (under 15 years.) My timidity and shyness started to fade and I began to make friends. I became the main contributor to the house in all the major games: hockey, football, and cricket and showed promise in gymnastics. I started to enjoy the importance and pampering and would often get help in the class, particularly in English, from the seniors.

Towards the end of the term, I was perpetually on drill by the Headmaster (the School had a Principal and a Headmaster, the latter second in position). My younger brother noticed that I was on the Headmaster's punishment list, and asked if I had wished the Headmaster (Mr. S.C.

Cowell) on his birthday. I said 'no,' "Well, the whole school did and you are the only one who didn't." I told him in villages nobody knows about birthdays and therefore I was not aware about the Headmaster's birthday; in fact, I did not know my own!

The next year I remembered and when the clock struck midnight, I was knocking the on door of the Headmaster's house. He opened thinking there was an emergency but saw me and before he could say anything, I said, "Sir, Wishing you a very, very happy birthday"! He was so surprised and taken aback that he gave me a bear hug! I could see his eyes moist, and after that, for the rest of the term I could get away with anything.

The next year, 1952. The students increased and therefore Shivalik and Vindhya houses were added to the existing Himalaya and Nilgiri. We formed lines and four Housemasters were asked to pick boys. The Himalaya Housemaster, Mr. Evans' first choice was Raj Sircar who was then the Head Boy – I was his second choice even though I was only in L IV (7th) class. On Raj Sircar's asking him about selecting me, Mr. Evans said, "Mark my words, this boy is going to win us the Cock House (best performing House)". His words proved to be prophetic!

On the playground, I performed exceptionally well but in class, English still set me back. To judge the general standard of the school, the English paper for each class was set by the Principal and corrected by him, whereas the Mathematics paper was set and corrected by the Headmaster. In the maths paper, I scored the highest, but failed in English. The Headmaster, who had become very fond of me, often helped me in English and told me, "Now that you speak fluently, why don't you write the way you speak"?

Movies screened in the known Barn Hall (named after one of the principals who contributed a lot in setting up the school). Normally the movies were westerns or war fare and those based on stories by Charles Dickens. Since we were a co-educational school, boys and girls sat together in class and interacted closely during house plays (drama) where they wrote the script, directed, acted and set up the stage. This was done with great effort and enthusiasm as there was a keen competition between the Houses and the points won would be counted towards the Cock House award.

The other interaction with the girls was at socials where music and dancing together was allowed. The teachers also took part.

I took a fancy for Charles Dickens after seeing movies based on his novels. His *A Tale of Two Cities* had a great impact on me emotionally and psychologically. It only strengthened my thinking to do anything for my friends or even others. I was particularly affected by the sacrifice Sydney Carton made for Charles Darnay who had been sentenced to death. Sydney Carton used his remarkable resemblance to Charles Darnay to save him and thus sacrificed his life for Lucie Monette, the lady he loved immensely but who married Charles Darnay. The words that Sydney Carton said to himself before his death, *'It is a far, far better thing that I do than I have ever done; it is a far, far rest I go to than I have ever known.* I read this book at least five times if I remember correctly!

The Principal is like a father figure but it is the Headmaster who actually runs the school. Mr. Cowell, the Headmaster, was a strict disciplinarian, yet he had a great sense of humour. Some of his habits can never be forgotten. Like, the day he removed his overcoat meant change to summer uniform – never mind if it was still cold. Similarly, the day he put on his overcoat meant winter uniform, even if the temperature was still high. His other peculiar habit was that his rounds would follow the same route and same time to the minute, or even seconds, each day. If anyone bunked a particular event and if he saw you, you had it – the drill! So we all knew if we were to bunk during his rounds, we made sure we were not seen. He had a dog named Vandy, who was a great warning system as she would walk way ahead of Mr Cowell if he was angry. This meant that his daily address would be an angry outburst followed by a joke. Similarly at prep, Vandy would take the lead to wake up anyone who had fallen sleep. But the most touching scene was when we left on our winter break from Dharampur railway station by three special trains. Mr Cowell and Vandy would come to see us off and we could see their tears; Vandy would sit on her hind legs and keep her paws up.

The year was 1953. My annual report showed that while progress at the sports was developing at a high rate, it was still low in the class room, especially in English. My House, Himalaya, was very happy as I was a major contributor towards the overall performance. Though I was still in class VIII, I became part of the 'brains trust', an integral part of policy, planning, and strategy of the House.

In 1954, Himalaya House won the Cock House and my contribution towards winning was acknowledged. We were confident of scoring/winning in all games except soccer, in which Nilgiri House was very strong with six of its players in the school team, whereas I was the only Himalaya boy in it. Vindhya and Shiwalik each had two players. The soccer match between Himalaya House and Nilgiri House needs special mention as it went down as historic and was talked about for many years. Psychologically, we had accepted that we could never win in soccer against Nilgiri. I deviated from normal setting of 5 3 2 1 and set up as 4 3 3 1, purely as a defensive to draw the match. Luckily, in the first half there was no score with Nilgiri missing several chances, and we were motivated towards drawing the game. When just 10 minutes left, our back, Angrish, kicked from the centreline. The Nilgiri house goal keeper was in two minds whether to take the ball before it bounced or after, resulting in the ball going over his head into the goal. The last whistle saw us as winners by one goal!

I met our soccer coach, Mr. Dasgupta, a former West Bengal state player, in his office. He wanted to know what strategy I had planned against Nilgiri, the strongest team. He appreciated it.

After a successful year at Sanawar, particularly on the playground and Himalaya House making me into a hero for winning the football trophy and the Cock House, I was on cloud nine. I left for home for the winter break feeling on the top of the world.

I regained my self-confidence, and started to enjoy the importance I was getting. Being adjudged the best school gymnast gave a further boost to my personality. It also confirmed my belief that whatever the background one came from, one has to find one's own identity I found mine.

Lessons from School and Early Challenges

Soccer Match with Kitchen Staff

The kitchen staff was mad about soccer. Each year they eagerly awaited the soccer season to play a match against the school team. They loved the game so much that the soccer team was the most pampered in the dining hall. The soccer season had barely started when Robin (the cook-cum-waiter, was the captain of the kitchen soccer team), would constantly ask me, "*Baba VS, hamara match kab ho ga*?" (Even though I was the junior-most in the team.) It is very difficult to explain their love for the game.

Cricket Match with Teaching Staff

Winning or losing the cricket match against the teaching staff was never the highlight; it was watching Mr. T.C. Kemp coming in to bat. I can never forget how the whole school would be present not to cheer the school team but to watch Mr. Kemp. The applause he received when he stepped out of the pavilion onto the field – Gurkha hat on, bat under his left armpit, gloves in his right hand, wearing his glasses – was deafening! At the crease, he would look at the umpire and ask for stumps, centre first, then the leg, and marked them with chalk kept behind the stumps. The pitch had a mat. After the stumps had been marked, he would wipe his glasses, don the gloves, glance at around the field and then gesture that he was ready. Mr. Kemp was always admired and we as kids loved this *nakhra*! (Mr. Kemp was the chemistry teacher, and if anyone was found dozing, you could be sure to be hit with a chalk like an unguided missile!)

Drill

Punishment was given by the prefects and sometimes by the headmaster. One of the drills was to go down to the Barn Field (playground) where there were 196 steps, touch the wall on the outer side and return within five minutes. Only a few could achieve this. (I happened to be one.)

Ice Cream

We were allowed to go to Kasauli once a month on a Sunday. The big attraction was the ice cream at the Alatia Hotel. Those days there were no cars or traffic on the road from Sanawar to Kasauli; we would take the short cut, I remember I would make it to the hotel in 21 minutes. Today one can take up to an hour by car. If any boy came down with the flu, her/his temperature had to be normal for 48 hours before being discharged. Once when I was down with flu and admitted in the school hospital. My temperature was normal for a day. The next day being a Sunday and the monthly Kasauli visit, I persuaded the doctor to let me go. Dr. Soin said, "My boy, if I let you go, you will be back in hospital". He allowed me and sure enough I returned with high fever.

Khud Cleaning, Pine Collection, and Home Day

Khud cleaning was a ritual each year to remove fallen pine needles in order to prevent *khud* fires around the school. It was always great fun. The pine cones collected were used in the fire place in our dormitory on Home Day (1 December every year); we did not sleep that night in the excitement to go home!

Dagru Picnic

The Dagru picnic on Easter Sunday was one of the school big events to which everyone looked forward. The main attractions were the cycles from Dharampur and, of course, the food!

Hike to Mt. Chore (highest peak in Shimla Hills)

During Easter holidays, Gurpal Inder Singh, Brijender Bala, Gurdev Purewal, Chhater Pati Singh, Narender Yadav and I planned a hike to Mt. Chore which is highest peak in Shimla Hills (14,000 feet). The Principal allowed us if escorted by a teacher. We approached Mr. Saleem Khan, our history teacher and cricket coach. Since I was the only among us in the school cricket team, I was asked to request him to come with us; to which he readily agreed. We carried our food, mainly tinned stuff and sleeping bags. It was really memorable and adventurous. Mr. Saleem Khan was very handsome, six feet tall and a Holkar cricket player. Our English teacher had a liking for Mr. Saleem Khan so on my essay on this hike, I heaped praises on Mr. Khan. That is the only time I passed in English!

Mastu, the Medical Assistant

Mastu, the medical assistant, was our great friend and never failed us. If your friend from GD (Girl's Department) was admitted in hospital, Mastu was always there to help us. My younger brother, Aman, and his friends, J.P. Singh and Ashok Seth, helped their friend, Chander Mohan, go home as he was homesick. They got him admitted to hospital but then put him on the train at Dharampur to catch the train to Delhi. The school learnt about this escapade only when a telegram came from his father saying 'Son safe in Delhi'. The school was shocked! The powers-that-be tried to find out who had helped him but failed. No tattling!

Special Trains from Dharampur Railway Station

Going home was always exciting and more so by train. Those days we went in school parties in three special trains. The exciting part was getting on and off and catching up with it on the next bend or around a small hill, reaching Kalka Railway Station and then shifting to another special train to Delhi. Of course, the most touching part was seeing Mr. S.C. Cowell with Vandy, both with tears trickling down their cheeks and Vandy with her paws raised.

PAYBACK – SANAWAR

The best gift my parents gave me was to put me into one of the finest institution in the country, Lawrence School Sanawar. The only way I could pay them back was to put my children in the same institution.

The belief of my parents that nothing is greater than to provide the best education to their children, in spite of the financial constraints, their will, their sacrifices and every effort they put in to impart the best education to their children.

After joining the Indian Air Force, started to put away certain portion of my salary to build a corpus to be able to afford the education of my children to the same institution, (Sanawar) and to overcome the problem of admission I registered both my sons at birth for class 6th.

I noticed that my wife's complete life started to revolve around her kids with total devotion to her sons and attached, therefore I will find it difficult in convincing her to send her sons to a residential school even if it's the best. She adjusted well with the extensive social activities of the squadron but her priority remained her sons.

I then decided to introduce Sanawar during founders of 1975 when Dr Harish Dhillon (my younger brother's classmate) was the headmaster and his sister Yogindra was my classmate.

The Founders at Sanawar is celebrated from 2nd to 4th October each year. We arrived a day earlier to take my wife around the school spread over 138 acres, lush green beautiful hill top. We then called on the headmaster in his palatial house overlooking the Sanawar valley. My wife was overwhelmed by the pampering she received by the headmaster and his sister Yogindra who was present then.

We then witnessed all the functions which are of very high standard professionally executed, from the facilitation of silver and golden batches, to tea at headmaster's residence, torch light tattoo, school plays (drama) inter house athletics meets, trooping the school colours during NCC parade and the OS (old Sanawarian) social evening (dinner dance) The applause the school band receives when the band march passes the audience and the bandmaster throws his mace in the air for 3 turns, it's just marvellous. Nostalgic.

We return home and asked my wife if she would like to send her sons to this excellent institution. It was a prompt reply to say YES even if I have work to manage the finances. (Battle won)

We did send both our sons to one of the finest institution Lawrence School Sanawar, the motto 'NEVER GINE IN' The Best School of All. (and pay back to our parents and their sacrifices)

Dropout from Sanawar

The year 1954 was probably the best of my life. I was the star of my House for winning them the Cock House and the Soccer Cup (which was the talk of the school for many years, as we beat the best and strong team). I also was adjudged the best gymnast of the school, competing against seniors. I was part of the school hockey team and the school cricket XI. At inter-house athletics on Founder's Day, I won three events – long jump, high jump, and 200 yards' I came second in 100 yards.

Thus, when I went home during the winter break, I left behind my meekness/timidity and was no more the *dhaull.* I was dying to meet my old friends in the village to tell them all how proud I was.

At home, mother was the first to notice that I was talking much more and that too with confidence. I was mixing well with my siblings. She told Father, "Vijai has changed a lot and is looking very good. I am very happy to see the change in him."

My father had shifted into the room that *Tauji*, Capt. Hari Singh, occupied before he moved to Rewari with his family. I often shared that room with Father.

One day, I came across some old letters strung on a string against the wall. Some were to *Tauji* and a few to my father. They were mainly from their British officers. One letter addressed to my father in Urdu caught my eye. My curiosity aroused, I read it, and was shocked, terrified, and angry. The letter was from my cousin's husband, demanding the return of a loan. It was so rude and humiliating. I was very surprised, distressed, and disappointed, because this cousin of mine had always treated me like her real brother and to save their land from ceiling restrictions they had transferred a part in my name. I was so disturbed mentally that I receded into my original self. The memorable year at Sanawar retreated, as if it was a dream.

I was disturbed to learn that the money had been borrowed to pay our school fees. In a flashback I realised the truth. I suddenly knew why only my younger brother was to be sent to Sanawar. It was because of money and not what I had thought. I noticed my mother was not wearing the gold chain she was very possessive about, as it was a gift from her *nani.* Whenever I enquired about it, she would be evasive. Once I even heard her say that that Vijai was very sensitive and he should never come to know. I learnt later that all her jewellery had been sold off to pay our school fees. I felt awful.

I was so shattered that all that had happened in school in 1954 became history. I told my father to withdraw me. He was confused as I had come back so happy. I explained that I was overage for my class and would like to sit for matriculation privately and then try for NDA; even then, I would have only one chance because of my age. He saw the point and agreed.

The school was taken aback. The withdrawal, coming on the heels of my performance, was totally unexpected. My housemaster, Mr. Evans and the sports teacher were very disappointed. They told my father that I had great potential, particular in sports.

I went back to my original self, but worked hard and passed the matriculation examination of Panjab University. I then moved to Delhi with my elder brother who was posted there to join a college to prepare to join Delhi University and subsequently apply for the NDA exam.

Chapter Three

The Path to the Uniform

College Days in Delhi (1955–56)

I got admission in Delhi College, Delhi, for preparatory class for entrance to Delhi University in the sports quota. My first shock came when I failed in the UPSC exam for NDA. Next, I failed in the preparatory exam for Delhi University. I left the college to prepare for UPSC direct entry to the Air Force Flying College (Academy). Though I passed the UPSC, I failed with the Air Force Selection Board in the next two attempts. My younger brother, on my advice, did matriculation in 1955–56 and passed the NDA exam. He was selected by the Services Selection Board in his very first attempt.

My multiple failures left me completely dejected and demoralised. I even forgot that I had been some kind of a star in school. I was back into my shell. I was completely lost as to what my next action should be. I was confused and almost at breaking point. I often used to pick up my nephew from St. Columbus School where he was studying. Their sports teacher, Brother Hugh, had learnt about my sports activities and so requested if I could take part in the Delhi Olympics on their behalf. I agreed only for the long jump. Why I mention this is that I was reminded of the legendary Sir Jesse Owens' during his visit to Delhi remarks at the National Sports Club of India while he saw me practising. That was in 1956. He asked me to jump again twice more and asked me my age. I was then 16. He told me I had a very good style and advised me to strengthen my thighs. This reminded me of a similar remark by the Maharaja of Patiala when he was the Chief Guest at Sanawar at our athletics meet. It was a confirmation of what my sports teacher had said. These comments surely were a temporary boost for a few moments, but my mind was still reeling. I really did not know what to do.

Failing to qualify for Delhi University, for the National Defence Academy and failing twice with the Air Force Selection Board put me under severe stress. My younger brother's selection to NDA made me feel that I was the black sheep of the family; guilt preyed on my mind. Though my brother and *bhabhi* (sister-in-law) always stood by me, I knew they were worried. I then suddenly felt very lonely. That night I grappled with dark thoughts about where I stood with my family. In that confused state, I decided to go back to the village and spend some time with my mother, though I still had a few more chances to appear for the Indian Air Force. However, I left for the village the next day.

After reaching the village I received message from Gurdev to visit his village. Did he learn about my multi failure.

Two Years in the Village: Getting to Know my Parents

After multiple failures, to be with my parents was a blessing in disguise. Getting to know them up from up close has been one of the greatest boons I could have and I cherish the experience. It can never forget their simplicity, high ideals and deeply rooted beliefs.

Mother (1957–58)

The two years stay with my mother was historic, as we four brothers had really not stayed enough there to really get to know her. God gave me this opportunity. The *gyan* (learning) I received then was a blessing in disguise, even though it was the result of multiple failures. I thank God for those failures. I say with confidence that the *gyan* I received during my stay with my mother could never have given to me in the best universities of the world.

My Learning about and from my Mother

She always knew my mental state, especially when I went through the phase of feeling disillusioned and believing I was a failed son. She involved me in her daily routine. I saw how attached she was to animals and noticed her buffaloes would take their feed only if my mother was present. Her complete life was devoted to her children. She would always be ready to cook what we were fond of. She enjoyed our visits, and looked forward anxiously for their visit.

During one of the festivals she called the family *panditji* to know about the *puja* and the timing. Overhearing them I learnt 'Not to accept anything that had not been earned.'

Every day there was something new to learn. One day she told me the ill effects of anger and greed. (There are three gates to hell: Lust, Anger, and Greed – and these corrupt the soul.)

She would often tell me, "You have been passionate as a child but, to elaborate, remember *compassionate* is when the blind can see and the deaf can hear". Each day taught me something new.

While imbibing all she said, I observed her keenly. I noticed that she had frequent severe headaches. She would always say it was nothing but simple gastric and that she had taken *methi-ki-phanki* and would soon be fine. On one occasion, she was grinding flour (*chaki pisna*) early in the morning when she had a severe headache. Her answer was the same – *methi-ki-phanki*. Whatever her health, she would go all out to ensure that her children, when visiting her, enjoyed their favourite food that she took all pains to make.

Though she knew everything about her children, we knew nothing about her even when we had grown up. We took her for granted and accepted all the comfort she provided. We learnt only when she suffered a paralytic attack that she had been living with high blood pressure. We were so involved in our own affairs – our jobs, our children – that we totally forgot about her frequent 'headaches'.

Those two years made me realise my mother's heart of gold. She has been the bedrock of my existence and has shaped me into what I am. She epitomises strength, compassion, patience, and stability – virtues that makes her nothing short of extraordinary. Her love, a universal language, speaks directly to the heart – transcending the barriers of speech and cognition. I quote an Arabic verse *Al-Jannatu Tahta Aqdamil Ummahet,* meaning: "Paradise exists at the feet of mother". The verse is shown below:

heaven lies under the feet of mothers

Thank you, Mother!

My Mother's Concern

My mother was concerned that I should not lose my self-esteem/self-respect, she was worried that mentally I should not accept for being unworthy, after my failures visa-vise with the success of my other siblings.

My mother strongly felt that only if the Air Force Selection Board had peeped into my son (that's me) they would have found Gold, *Woh Jhank ke tho Dekhte.*

Getting to Know My Father

My father being the youngest of the siblings in a big *zamindar* family, suddenly matured after the family was deprived of their property; yet, certain traits remained.

From lavish food to a poor man's diet! (*teekra* and *pyaz ki ganthee*). No food from friends or cousins could tempt him even though he was hungry; he preferred the simple fare the rest of the family was having. His father had died when he was still very young but his brother saw potential in him, and sent him to a school in Rewari. He settled well and became an active participant in sports and other activities in the school.

Mentally and physically, he stood out among his peers – always ready to do more. One incident stands out. It was the custom for the entire school to go to a renowned *ashram* to dredge or clean the water pond that had dried up in the summer. The dredged sludge was to be shaped into mud cakes and each child was expected to make one. For this, every child was given one *ladoo*, but my father would always make two mud cakes and then demand two *ladoos*. Amused at this, the *seer* (monk) supervising the pond cleaning asked him to fight a *kushti* (wrestle) with the ashram seers. Only if he won, would he be rightfully entitled to two *ladoos*! My father wrestled the *seer* to the ground and won; rightfully claiming his two *ladoos*!

My father, sensitive as he was, understood the financial condition of the family. He left school without his mother and brother knowing and joined the army as it needed recruits because of the First World War.

He was fairly ambitious and worked sincerely and honestly. He would go out of his way to help newly commissioned British officers. He would appraise them about local festivals, customs, beliefs, and the language. In those days, the Hyderabad Infantry Regiment (now the Kumaon Regiment) recruited men from three castes/classes: Kumaoni, *Ahirs* and Jats. This was the case with his Battalion too.

The selection to JCO (now Junior Commissioned Officers) was a huge promotion for an Army soldier; it was the highest rank one could aspire for in those days. The promotion as per the policy was caste-wise by turn. It so happened that when my father became eligible, it was then the turn of an Ahir who was qualified for it. But the Subedar Major, who was of a different caste, was keen to promote someone from his own community. He detailed my father to be the guard commander at the Brigade Commander's residence. This particular Brigade Commander was known to sack guard commanders for any mistake – real or imagined. My father was quick to understand the situation and appraised his company Commander. He requested that he be allowed to choose his men and have new uniforms issued. He selected his guard – all six feet tall (he himself was a six-footer plus with an athletic body). He duly reported at the residence of the Brigade Commander and found that he was away for sports. As soon as the Brigade Commander's vehicle neared his official bungalow, my father gave the cautionary word of command. My father had a loud, commanding voice. On hearing that drill command, the Brigade Commander got off his jeep and marched towards the guard post outside his house. When he was about 30 metres away, my father gave the general salute command. The Brigade Commander looked at the Guard Commander up and down – perfect salute, perfect physical stature. He then looked straight into the eyes of the commander, and proceeded to inspect the guard. Instead of entering the house, he asked the battalion commander who that smart havildar was. When he was told about my father's record and that he was due for his promotion to JCO, he ordered that he be promoted and sent to a training centre where he would motivate the new recruits. My father got his promotion and was posted to the Regimental Centre (then at Agra).

When my father was selected for an officer's commissioning he was asked by his 2 I/C to turn reject the offer as he wanted him to be his Subedar Major of the battalion when he would be taking over (this was during WW II).

My father was Mentioned-in-Despatches and awarded the Order of British India (1st Class) which entitled him to write 'Sardar Bahadur' before his name. He was also granted land which he turned down.

After retirement my father worked for upliftment of the scheduled castes, helped their children to get better education, even got our own *mochi's* (cobbler's) son into government service (IAS).

My father had a commanding, loud voice. Whenever a cow or camel did not return from grazing, they would ask him to announce the loss which could be heard in surrounding villages!

Once, my father had a minor road accident and was admitted in the Army Hospital at Delhi Cantonment. I was then posted at Palam with the VIP Squadron and would visit my father daily. My father would tell me every day, "*Bhai tadke aawa go tho main mero pawu go*" (Bhai when you will come tomorrow you will find me dead). The doctor told me that my father was OK but under shock and low morale. We then transferred him to Ferozepur where my eldest brother was the GOC and there, with help of a Jat Regiment and with *hukka* and local tales, he was up and about in two days!

My father never raised his voice or hand at his children. He never called his children by name but addressed them as '*bhai*'. My parents made a perfect team when it came to raising their children. We are finding it very difficult to match them as parents ourselves.

Doctor Gurdev Purewal Orthopaedic Surgeon Trek to Rohtang Pass

Gurdev and I had grown up together as children. Remained best friends as adults, as parents, as grandparents. He would never fail in his duties towards society, friends, family. He was very a very compassionate doctor, dedicated and sincere. Wherever he went, he left a mark. Whomsoever he met became life time relationships. His passing has been a great loss to his family, his multitude of friends, associates and professional colleagues. I personally have lost a true friend and the world has lost a good human being.

I can never forget he was the one who helped me to adjust after joining Lawrence School Sanawar, and it was the beginning of a friendship for a lifetime. Though Gurdev was a class senior to me but we were always together in all the other school activities. Narender Yadav (who was from my village) joined us and then Vishnu Bhagwat, (Former Naval Chief) Ramesh Pratap Singh and Naresh Bahadur Singh bonded and we six became inseparable friends.

We both left school early to do matriculation privately. Gurdev joined pre-medical college in Amritsar and I joined a college in Delhi while staying with my brother. One day Gurdev landed up in Delhi unannounced and asked me, "Vijai have you heard of Kake Da Dhaba in Connaught Place I hadn't. "Well, Kake Da Dhabha, serves the best tandoori Chicken", he informed me. The year was 1956 and tandoori chicken those days (and even now, I suppose!) was most sought after. A few months later Gurdev was in Delhi again, this times he said that he would take me out to Pindi on Pandara Road as now they serve the best tandoori chicken in town. I started enjoying his surprise visits.

I remember Gurdev had an inclination towards becoming a Film Star. He invited his six School friends for a celebration to come to Delhi at my place for a dinner then most expensive restaurant Gaylord's in Connaught Place. Vishnu Bhagwat always a very serious type, told Gurdev that we were not going to eat till he told us where he got all that money. Gurdev told us that he had been signed as the hero in a Punjabi film and had received a generous advance – so we were celebrating. He wanted to know if there was anything wrong about it. Vishnu told him that everything was wrong. He made us collectively pay the bill and told Gurdev go and return the money he had received and forget becoming a film star. (In those days, films were not considered a good career). Vishnu then wrote to his brother, who then Colonel in the Indian Army was posted in Ranchi. We learnt later Gurdev joined Government Medical College in Amritsar and topped his class. He specialised as an Orthopaedic Surgeon and was posted to the Medical College in Rohtak.)

After he got admission to the Medical College in Amritsar, he left for his village for the summer break. He had learnt about my failures with Delhi College and did not clear the NDA exams and now failing twice with Air Force Selection Board living in the village. I suddenly get a message to reach Hoshiarpur by train, Gurdev received me with a hug and a firm handshake and left for his village by bus, received by all his family members affectionately.

In the evening went for walk in his fields where carried a knife, he picked naturally ripened melons which we ate while sitting next to a canal. I had never eaten such sweet melons again. While enjoying lovely surrounding with our feet in the canal water mentioned about the trek to Rohtang Pass, I knew that he was planning something like that as he had asked me to bring my Haver Sack. During all this while we never spoke about his admission the Medical College or my failures.

Tomorrow we will leave for Pathankot and from there to Joginder Nagar by train. From Joginder Nagar we will trek to Rohtang Pass via Mandi, Kulu and Manali, he said.

From Hoshiarpur to Pathankot one has to cross a river (I think river Bias). Even the bus had to be taken across the river by a ferry boat. It took us a full day to trek/walk from Joginder Nagar to Manali. At Manali there was not a soul there so we slept on bench in front of what it looked like to be a post office. We ate what packed food we had as there was not even a tea shop in sight.

The next morning, we saw that the weather was turning bad so we decided to abandon the trip to the Rohtang Pass and decided to head for our school via Narkanda and Solan. From Solan we took the bus to

Dharampur and walked to School. We were received so well and expressed disappoint for both of us having left the school early, Mr Evans my house master and football coach in particular. After meeting all the teaching and sports staff and the kitchen staff. Robin, the cook/bearer, met us with lot of love and affection, mentioned about the football we played together. We both left for Kalka to board the Kalka Mail. Gurdev was to change trains at Ambala for Hoshiarpur. It was such a great feeling to be in school again – nostalgic!

After a firm hand shake and a hug, we parted at Ambala. He had to take the connecting train, and I remained in the Kalka Mail to Delhi. As the train moved and I lay down on the berth thinking, why did Gurdev suddenly decide on the Rohtang trek? My mind pondered and a flash back, it could not be a co-incident that all my failure preceded his surprise visits, so was the Tandoori Chicken just an excuse and now Trek to Rohtang was to take my mind off for not succeeding with Indain Air Force. He intentionally chose the trek to Rohtang remembering my love and excitement when we did Trek to Mt Chore highest hill in Shimla Hills while we were at School. These very thoughts made me realise what my friend Gurdev is, the degree of concern inspiring, my heart swelled for him, do I really deserve such a friend. Gurdev I love you, I respect you from my heart.

When my father learnt that Gurdev was posted to Government Medical College & Hospital Rohtak, decided to go and meet him. On reaching the hospital, he enquired about Doctor Purewal. Baba (my father) was told that the Doctor was in the operation theatre. My father requested if a chit could be conveyed to him, which was done. Promptly Gurdev came out to hand over his room key and Baba was escorted to his room. Gurdev said he would join him within half an hour. Gurdev took my father out for lunch. Father asked him about his hair. (Earlier he supported a turban) "Oh it's a long story, my friends did not allow me to be a big film star", Gurdev laughed and said.

When it was time for my father to leave, Gurdev went to drop him to the bus stand in a cycle rickshaw. On the way, many people (from what my father told me- hundreds) kept coming and touching Gurdev's feet. Gurdev told Baba that the surrounding villages have done away with manual fodder cutting to electric machines, and as electricity supply was only at night, it was resulting in people dozing off and hence injuring or losing limbs. They would be brought to the hospital in a bad shape and that I he had been working day and night to save their limbs and lives. At the bus stop the *rickshaw walla* refused to accept money and insisted that he would drop the Doctor back to the hospital. My father felt so proud of him! He thanked him and told him that he was a greater hero than any screen star, the people of district Rohtak took him to be like a God. (My father tells me that the people in Rohtak were disappointed when Haryana became a state and Doctor Gurdev Purewal was transferred to Medical College Amritsar.)

Doctor Gurdev Purewal was appointed as the registrar at the Medical College Amritsar. He then requested if he could do post-graduation in Orthopaedics at the Royal Orthopaedic Hospital in Birmingham, UK. He was permitted and went to the UK for higher studies. He went on to top the course. During the course, he performed a very complicated knee surgery which caught the attention of the London Press. after reading this news, a leading Orthopaedic Hospital in America offered him a job which he turned down. After finishing his course, the Birmingham Hospital too offered him a job as they wanted him to stay on. He turned down the offer. so They then offered that he worked for two months and they would pay him for the full year and reimburse travel cost both ways. He could take two month leave, Gurdev found the offer attractive as he would still continue his job at Amritsar.

In Amritsar, Gurdev's subordinate requested if he could get him a seat for post-graduation at Birmingham. Gurdev helped his subordinate for a seat in the course at Birmingham Hospital, while his subordinate was dong the course realised Gurdev was working even though only two months in a year, which his subordinate informed the Govt of Punjab. The Govt. of Punjab punished him by demoting him and made his subordinate his boss. Gurdev was completely taken aback. The humiliation was too much to bear. What hurt him even more was that he had gone out of his way to help this guy. Gurdev wrote to the American Hospital if the offer they had made still stood. He received the job confirmation, with all formalities and the air ticket. Thereafter Doctor Gurdev Purewal disappeared and for many years the Govt. of Punjab, his friends, and most of his relatives were unaware of his whereabouts.

Due to his hard work and dedication, Doctor Gurdev Purewal became one of the most sought after doctors in and around Pittsburgh and Weirton, WV. where he lived in a palatial house. He had a single engine aircraft which he flew for pleasure every week. We renewed contact again in the year 1988 when he surprised me with a phone call while I was Station Commander Bombay.

My wife, I and our granddaughter visited him in 2013. What a time he and his wife Surrender gave us. We visited New York, Washington, Niagra Falls – the works. Thereafter we kept in touch, and I had told him that during his next trip to India that we would visit our old School, my village, the eye hospital and Leh (Ladakh) and visit the Gurdwara Pather Sahib.

His sudden demise was too much to bear. I can never forget him. He lives on in my heart.

Chapter Four

Taking Flight

Decision to Join the Army (1958)

It is said that the greatest journey occurs when we stand still.

I had failed to qualify for entrance to Delhi University for graduation; failed the NDA entrance exams and to add to that I had four failures to join the Indian Air Force. Therefore, I was deemed not qualified adequately/ educationally for an appropriate job in keeping with the family tradition.

It was an accepted fact that our eldest brother was not only the one who took major decisions; he also enjoyed unquestioned respect from the whole family including our parents. It was therefore considered his right to guide the family.

Considering the 'dead end' I was seen as boxed in, my eldest brother strongly recommended that I join the army as a recruit. The Kumaon Regiment was naturally chosen because it was father's regiment and the then Regimental Centre Subedar Major had been my father's trainee and the Centre Adjutant (Maj. C.L. Phogat) was my brother's classmate in K.G. School, Ajmer. The plan was that I attempt facing the army selection board through the ranks. This is generally done by those who find it difficult to clear the UPSC written exams or were over age. (Though I had cleared the UPSC exams for direct entry to the IAF.)

Actually, it was the selection board where I had a problem and not the UPSC exams. Therefore, I thought that joining the army as a recruit might not help as I still would have to face the Services Selection Board. Moreover, as a repeater, it would make things even more difficult. I could feel that the family was losing patience with me. They were concerned about my future. My multiple failures, not attending college for graduation, and not doing anything in the previous four years made the family desperate to see me doing something. Under the circumstances, joining the army as a recruit was considered to be the best option.

"Gum to likha so likha meri zindagi mein.
Yeh raat bhar neend na aana kis jurm ki saza hai"

غم تو لکھا سو لکھا میری زندگی میں
یہ رات بھر نیند نہ آنا کس جرم کی سزا ہے؟

RANIKHET: THE FIRST STEP (1959)

In life, certain memories remain very vivid. One such memory that I recall in minute detail occurred almost seven decades ago.

I was to report to Kumaon Regimental Centre at Ranikhet on Monday, 16 February 1959, for recruitment. I therefore had to leave our village, Sadat Nagar, on 15 February to board the train from Delhi Junction to Kathgodam and from there by bus to Ranikhet. Kosli was the nearest railway station to our village (about 5 km away). Since there were no means of transportation generally available, people either walked or went by camel/ bullock cart.

I was to catch the train at around three in the afternoon to Rewari to take the connecting train to Delhi to board the Nainital Express for Kathgodam.

Phulia (our help) brought the camel well in time to take me to the railway station. I decided to walk; my father (Baba) and *Phulia* said that they would like to see me off. Generally, there was nothing unusual about my taking a train and I always travelled alone. This time Baba and *Phulia* decided to accompany me to the station. Just before leaving, my mother said, *"Bhai, it is immaterial what one becomes but it is more important to be a good human being"*. I told her I would always remember that. (I could sense her mixed emotions, given that her two elder sons were already army officers, her youngest son was then at the National Defence Academy to become an army officer and here was this I leaving for the Kumaon Regimental Centre to become a jawan!)

A word about *Phulia* (he was a scheduled caste). *Phulia* was the Man Friday to Baba. Even though his primary duties were to take care of our land and the camel, he was very devoted and extremely loyal to the family. He always remained at Baba's side – through good times and bad. His loyalty was to the extent that he would give his life for the family. During my two years in the village, I often walked with *Phulia* and helped him prepare the feed for the camel. He developed a special liking for me and became very protective.

I was carrying just a small bag containing toiletries, underwear and one shirt, a pair of trousers and a pullover. *Phulia* carried the bag.

The five-kilometre walk to the railway station passed in silence. My mind was pre-occupied thinking of the kind of life that awaited me. By the time I reached the station I had come to terms with the position that I would have as an army recruit in the family. I recalled the words of my mother and felt at peace. Baba noticed it and gave an affectionate nod. I could see that *Phulia's* eyes were moist. He shook my hand with both of his and said, "*Bhai, apna khayal rekhna*" told him I will be fine. At Kathgodam, I was told that I could avail the vehicles of the Kumaon Regimental Centre that were there to pick up their men returning from leave/temporary duty. However, I preferred to take a public bus. To stop thinking about the future I admired the scenic beauty of the Kumaon hills.

I reported to the Centre Subedar Major at Ranikhet as briefed. He was waiting for me. I was handed over to the Recruiting Officer along with the other candidates present. After the preliminary tests, , the candidates were sent for medical examination. I recall the doctor asked me to do 50 sit-ups. On checking my heart rate thereafter, he scolded me for not having done the sit-ups. I told him, "Sir, I have done them". Not believing me, he told his assistant to make me do another 100 sit-ups which too I did. When he still found there was not much change in my heart beat, he looked at me and said, "No more medical required". I was asked to report at Dulikhet training area.

RECRUIT TRAINING AT DULIKHET

At Dulikhet I was asked to report to the Quarter Master Havildar, where I was issued with a complete kit/uniform and a plate, a mug and a spoon which became an integral part of me. I was allotted a bed in one of the barracks where the recruits were to stay. In the evening roll call by the Havildar Major, we were divided into smaller groups of eight to 10 and allotted an *ustad* (instructor – generally of the rank of a Naik), who was to remain with us for the rest of the training. We were given the weekly programme. A rifle (.303) was allotted to each one of us, which would be part of the uniform and we were explained how to maintain it. I was allotted 'C' (Charlie) Company.

Interacting with the recruits, I realised that practically all of them came from poor families and that their educational qualification was either class VIII or less.

A new chapter had begun in my life. I had no idea where it would take me.

At the very first morning PT, the *ustad* found I was extraordinarily good in 'horse' and ground work. He became fond of me, and promised that he would train me for the Services Gymnastics Team. (The instructor wanted to know where I had learnt PT/gymnastics. I told him that I was the best gymnast of my school.)

Seeing that I already knew all the drill movements with and without a rifle (I was part of the colour party NCC). I was marched before the company commander and the company subedar sahib. I was then tested again about drill movements, weapons – mainly .303 rifle and LMG (light machine gun) – map reading and my knowledge about the defence services. I was found satisfactory and promoted to the 35th week.

The Komola Camp centre farms are part of the training in the initial stage where they are expected to do farming. Since I was placed in the 35th week I was not sent there. All the personnel of the Centre participated in the annual firing. It so happened that my score in all the weapons (.303, LMG and small arms) with different targets was the best. The officer in charge of the firing range wanted to re-check my performance and made me fire at snap targets with both the .303 and LMG and found the result to be excellent. He shook my hand and congratulated me. The result was announced during the *Durbar*. I was asked to stand and was introduced to the Centre Commandant and all those present – a feat very rare for a recruit!

I was not included in the fatigue party detailed for cleaning/painting of the entire Centre, including the officer's accommodations, every afternoon. I was asked to report to the sports section as I was selected for the Centre's football and hockey teams.

After barely a few weeks I was asked to move in with four *jawans* (regular soldiers) who had arrived from their respective battalions for training to face the Services Selection Board. (This is rare as recruits have to complete their training before they can be recommended for such training.)

The five of us were shifted to a separate barrack. Our normal routine was to attend the morning PT; thereafter, an officer would explain interview techniques and the rest of the day was left to us for self-study.

One day we decided to see a movie in the Centre cinema hall. When we reached there, we saw a girl in a *burka* but with her face uncovered. She was extremely beautiful! We had heard of *Busra ki Hoorein* – well, we saw one in Ranikhet in her designer attire that day, with matching footwear, and the gait of a princess. Though we visited the cinema several times, we never saw her again.

Our normal dress was service trousers and a PT vest with a camp comforter used as a *muffler*. The Centre Adjutant hated anyone using the camp comforter as a *muffler*. Fortunately, he had a motor cycle without a silencer so when he started it, we knew it was time to hide the comforter.

Another ritual was the evening tea at the *Bania* shop. The owner was of our age and would join in the tea session. We would draw lots as to who would pay on any particular day. If the owner's name was drawn, he paid for the tea and we shared the cost of sweets and *samosas*.

At the inter-Company hockey tournament, I was selected to represent Charlie Company. We were to play against HQ Company. The Centre Adjutant who was the captain of the HQ Company team was believed to be a terror on the hockey field. I volunteered to play centre half to tackle him. He realised that he was being covered by me and that I was not allowing the ball to reach him. He threw me out of the team, saying that as I was no longer with Charlie Company; I was asked to be a referee. I answered in English to say I do not know how to be one. To this he said, "*Angrezi mei bolta hai aur referee karna nahi aata*". I quickly came to be known as the '*khas* recruit' (special recruit).

Capt. R.V. Jatar, Charlie Company commander, not only was fond of me but also monitored my progress. He inducted me and Krishnand Ghildayal (who was also going to face the Services Selection Board), into the officers' cricket team.

Ghildayal and I were ordered to accompany Capt. Jatar whenever he was required to survey a location or take an excursion among the Kumaon hills. On one such occasion, we were asked to report to him at 4:30 in the morning. We were waiting about 50-odd metres from his house when his wife came out. She saw us waiting. I told Ghildayal that most likely she would send us some tea; she did! (Many years later when I happened to meet the Jatars, I mentioned that mug of tea.)

Most of the *ustads* were very fond of me. I spent a lot of time with them learning and seeking advice and guidance on every aspect of the training.

A very prestigious football tournament between the training centres of the Indian Army was to be held at Lucknow. I was lucky to be selected for the Kumaon Regiment Centre team. While waiting to be picked up from my billet, the centre commandant came on inspection, accompanied by the centre adjutant, the centre subedar major and the Charlie Company commander. He noticed me and was informed who I was and that I was leaving for Lucknow.

Suddenly, I found myself not only taken off the football team, but removed from the selection board training and sent to join the regular recruit training. I learnt later that there was a complaint against me to the

Chief of Army Staff, Gen. Thimmayya, by his Subedar Major when he was commanding 4 Kumaon. It was that I was being given special treatment whereas his son was being treated as any other normal recruit, including being sent to the Komola Camp from which I had been excused.

My removal from the football team, cadre (officer) training and being sent back to normal recruit training became the general talk of the centre. Yet, all the *ustads* treated me with utmost respect and generally asked me to take the class.

After having passed the UPSC exams for commissioning into the Indian Air Force flying branch, I was ordered to report at the Air Force Selection Board at Dehradun. I was selected and found medically fit. I was to report at Air Force Flying College, Jodhpur, towards the end of November 1959.

I returned to Ranikhet to complete the formalities to take a discharge from the Centre. By then, word had spread about my selection as an officer in the Indian Air Force. Almost all the instructors, fellow recruits, and those undergoing cadre training congratulated me.

I owe everything that happened at Ranikhet to Capt. R.V. Jatar, who retired as a Brigadier. He constantly watched my progress and ensuring that I always got my due. I also feel he played a major part in restoring my self-confidence which probably helped me to clear the AF Selection Board after four unsuccessful attempts.

I thanked the Centre Adjutant and the Centre Subedar Major who helped in my induction into the Regiment. They expressed their happiness at my selection to the IAF and mentioned that I had left a big mark on every aspect of recruit training including sports. I thanked them and bid farewell to all my *ustads* – especially the PT, Drill, and the Firing Range *Ustads*. They were so happy to see me and said, "*Aap ka jaisa recruit na abhi tak koi aaya aur na hi kabhi aaye ga*".

I bid farewell to my colleagues who were to face the selection board and wished them all the best. (They were all selected.)

Finally, before leaving, I went and profusely thanked Capt. R.V. Jatar for all that that he had done for me and told him that he had played a big role in my selection. He wished me good luck for my training at Jodhpur, and said that he would remain in touch. We continue to be in touch with each other till today.

I was to leave for Kathgodam by civil bus to catch a train for Delhi. Quite a few fellow recruits, firing range *ustad* and my colleague officer trainees came to see me off at the bus stand. I profusely thanked the company subedar sahib and the centre jamadar adjutant sahib (now naib subedar) for taking all the trouble to see me off.

I was surprised to see the PT *Ustad*, the drill *Ustad* and recruit Shinde at Kathgodam railway station. I profusely thanked them and told them how touched I was by this great gesture of theirs. Both the *ustads* said with one voice, "*Arey sahibji! Aap ne tho Ranikhet mai ek misal kayam kar di! Na aisa koi recruit kabhi aaya aur na hi kabhi aaye ga. God bless you*".

Recruit Shinde told me that he told his father about me. His father had sent his blessings and said he would always add my name during his daily prayers. Shinde was the first recruit I interacted with in Ranikhet. His bed was next to mine. I learnt that he came from a backward area of Maharashtra from a very poor family. I found him to be very quiet. He kept to himself, but was eager to learn and was very hard working. After I moved to officer training, he often came to meet me.

One day Shinde came looking highly distressed. When I asked him what was wrong, he said that stipend had been delayed and needed to send a money order to his father that day itself. Fortunately, I had some cash so we both went to the post office to send the MO. He thanked me profusely and I told him to come to the *Bania* shop after fatigue/sports and we would have tea together. The kind of stress I saw in him made me feel I should know more about him and his family and whether I could be of any help.

I ordered the favourite *samosas* and *khowa ki burfi* and learnt that Shinde had not come to the *Bania* shop for the last seven-eight months. Asked why, he said all the money he got he sent home without keeping any for himself. He felt comfortable with me and opened up about his family.

He said, "You know, Vijai Bhai, we come from that part of Maharashtra which is backward and drought prone and we have a very small land holding. On many days we go to sleep hungry. I was keen to pursue my studies but seeing the condition of the family, I had to work as a labourer. My parents are weak and fragile. I also have a younger brother and sister to support. Being recruited into the Indian Army has been Godsend for me".

He continued, "The reason I send money every month is that it makes me feel comfortable to know that my parents won't sleep hungry. I hope I never fail my duty towards my parents, my younger brother and sister and never give them a chance to be disappointed with me."It was a very difficult parting. Words were hardly spoken, only feelings were exchanged. I saw them waiting for the last *bogey* to disappear from sight. It was a great learning from Shinde and he left a lasting impact on me.

Although the train had left the station, I kept standing at the door, my eyes moist looking out at nowhere. The period of my failures was a great boon as I spent two years with my parents, imbibing their ethos. My nine months stay at Ranikhet too was a great experience. It was enjoyable and it is there that I witnessed and felt true human relationships. These two years and nine months were the best years of my life.

I went to sleep determined to get up the next morning and start a new chapter of my life.

I have learned that no phase of life is ever truly bad, because perhaps God has something better in store for us.

Postscript

I may mention that after training at Ranikhet I was to be drafted to Charlie Company of 13th Battalion, The Kumaon Regiment, who were then located in Ladakh. Before I could be drafted I was selected for the Indian Air Force. I was therefore destined not to join (all *Ahirs*) who, under the legendary Major Shaitan Singh, Param Vir Chakra (Posthumous), laid down their lives fighting the Chinese in 1962 to the last man and to the last bullet at Rezang La in 1962. Who knows what fate has in store!

I may quote verse 2:47 of the Bhagwad Gita that the **Adhikar** (the rightful scope of human effort) is limited to **Karma**, and the **Phal** (reward) or the result is for destiny to determine.

Chapter Five

Trials, Duty, and Life's Twists

AIR FORCE FLYING COLLEGE, JODHPUR

I was to report at Jodhpur by end November 1959 for the 79th pilot course which commenced in January 1960. All direct entry cadets were asked to report a month in advance (cadets from NDA joined when the course began). We were received at the Jodhpur railway station by a handsome Flight Lieutenant wearing a T-shirt, well ironed trousers, and fancy foot wear (Kolhapuri *chappals*). We were *maha* impressed! We learnt later that he was an instructor nicknamed Gabu (he resembled film star Raj Kapoor, and retired later as an Air Marshal and settled at Dehradun).

In one month till the course began, we were taught drill movements, mess etiquette, how to pay compliments to officers, and were ragged a bit by senior flight cadets. The physical ragging was light and consisted of either push-ups or-sit ups. Another kind of ragging was actually 'professional' – shaving off the middle of one's hair making a runway on the head or if one sported a moustache, it would be shaved on one side to resemble the half wings that are worn by navigator officers! The aim was to direct our focus on flying, because if one didn't make the grade within the specified number of hours, one could be sent home or, if one was lucky, could continue in the Air Force by being sent for a navigation course. I had a ragging session with Senior Flight Cadet Clarrie D'Lima, with whom I later became friends and we served together in the VIP squadron. (It was unfortunate that he was the captain of that ill-fated Tu-124 aircraft that crashed with Prime Minister Mr. Morarji Desai was on board; the Prime Minister survived but sadly, the crew did not.)

1st Row, Left to right: R. Singh, Lt. Gill, F/O Chakraverty, Lt. Choudhry, Roach
Middle Row: Patro, Yadav, Anukul, Ratnaparki, Mahendale
Last Row: Ghosh, Dhall, Ranganath and Dias

Just before supper, when we were not doing night flying, we usually gathered in the cadets' mess either gossiping, discussing our flying sorties or listening to the radio (no TV those days). On one occasion, the Beatles' song 'Hard Day's Night' was playing on the radio. It was immediately switched off. Similarly, on another occasion, the Dev Anand song '*Hum bekhudi mein tumko pukare chale gaye*' was also switched off. As the story went, whenever these songs were played on the radio, there always was either an incident or an accident. It may be a coincidence; however all of us – whether superstitious or not, believed in it.

We were assigned to three different flights after extensive ground training and checks. Procedures and emergencies memorised, our training flying commenced with flying instructors. There are three stages of flying. The basic was on the HT-2 aircraft, the inert stage was on T6 G (Harvard) and the final was on Vampire jets. Once the cadets made the grade in all these stages, they were commissioned in the Indian Air Force as officers in the flying branch. Those who were sent for transport flying were sent for training on DC3 Dakota, and those flying fighters were sent for advance training at Hakimpet.

Basic Training at Air Force Flying College, Jodhpur

My basic training commenced. I was allotted Flt. Lt. Mangat as my instructor and my co-pupil was Flt. Cadet Sonpar. After a few training sorties and debriefings, I learnt that F/C Sonpar was a born flyer and was ready to go for his first solo flight way before completing the laid down syllabus, whereas I was still struggling and made my first solo within just about minimum hours required. Though progress was slow, it was not enough reason for suspension. Flt. Lt. Mangat liked Sonpar for his flying ability and me for my good nature and hard work and would spend more time on me than Sonpar. Just when I began showing a lot of improvement, Mangat was posted out and we both were to be allotted new instructors.

We knew that one of us would be allotted an instructor who was known among cadets as the 'killer'. He had already suspended two cadets and two naval officers. I being a borderline case, there was no way I could escape being thrown out. I prayed the whole night that Sonpar should go to the new instructor. If I went to him, there was no chance of my survival. As luck would have it, it was I who went to him and my ordeal began.

His reputation, my slow progress and the chief instructor (who was known to always suspend whoever was put up to him) was a perfect combination for my suspension.

It was customary for pupils to report to their instructors. After a sleepless night, I prepared to face my new instructor – my uniform starched, cap buttons 'brassoed', trying desperately to look smart which I thought would create a good impression. I ran to report to my new instructor, showing lot of enthusiasm and gave him a smart salute. Yet, the bomb fell – "You f***** bastard, why do I have to see your dirty/filthy face first thing in the morning?" He continued to scold me not only with the choicest of abuses but in all the languages he knew. By now I was terrified and in shock; my body trembled. If he had carried on for one more minute, I would have collapsed.

Next morning, when I heard that my instructor was coming towards the cadets' crew room, I ran and hid in a cupboard. He asked for me and I came out. As soon as he saw me, the abuses began. He then accused me of not reporting to him! *Each night was a nightmare and dreaded the morning.*

This trauma continued and each morning I waited as to when I would be put up for suspension. My friends/course mates would console and reassure me that after all, the Air Force was not the only option. (It was a foregone conclusion that I would be suspended, the only question was when?)

How I performed the routine, (flying sorties) I have no idea. I would climb into the cockpit trembling and under severe stress. There was no briefing or de-briefing, only abuses.

When I read in the SRO (Station Routine Order) that the Chief Instructor was going on leave and that Sqn. Ldr. Lalkaka would officiate in his place, I thought my condition would be better as Lalkaka never suspended any one put up to him – he always gave one more chance with a change of instructor. I prayed and prayed that my instructor put me up for suspension while Lalkaka was officiating as the Chief Instructor.

I was so excited to see that I was programme to fly with Sqn. Ldr. Lalkaka the next day. I thanked God for hearing to my prayers. I was quite confident that he would give me a chance with a change of instructor. The evening earlier, my friends congratulated me and briefed me on all the checks, procedures and emergencies and wished me the best of luck. Sqn. Ldr. Lalkaka in his briefing told me that it would be just like any other training sortie. In the de-briefing, I could make out that he was happy with my performance. He shook hands with me and said, "You have passed". I thanked him and said, "I hope, Sir, you will give me a change of instructor." He said No, when you will return from your summer break you will have the same instructor. I was totally confused and told my friends I thought I had survived suspension. When they told me it had been actually my final test, I just could not believe it! I looked at the programme again – it did say it was the final test. I was so stressed that I had read it as a suspension check. (I now firmly believe God exists – it was only His blessings that saw me through. Or was there some one praying for me somewhere, most likely my mother!)

Since I had passed my final test, I was no longer required to go to the flight office. There were still a few weeks before the summer break and several cadets were yet to finish their training. Though I never went to the flight office, just the name of my instructor was enough to give me the shivers. I therefore went for a swim every morning.

One day while at the swimming pool I saw my instructor and my blood drained out with fear. I tried to stay under water to avoid him and swam the length of the pool under water just to be away from him. Finally, he called out to me and told me to see him in his office.

I cursed my luck while dressing and remembered a cadet who was suspended after he had finished his final test. I was sure to meet the same fate. Probably my instructor was not happy about my final test; I feared I would not be considered for either a navigation course or for the ground duty branch and therefore be asked to leave. I thought about my mother who had gone through severe stress during my multiple failures and I had heard her once telling my father as to when will this son of hers would see the dawn, as the sun was refusing to rise for me. I knew my suspension at this stage would devastate her. Mentally I was already telling her, *"Mother I am very sorry and I truly believe that I do not deserve to be your son. Please forgive me."*

I reached the flight office and requested permission to enter. I heard my instructor reply in a soft voice. Neither did he shout nor did he hurl any abuses; I was surprised! Yet, I was trembling. "Come and sit down, my son", he said. I remained standing. "Will you have tea?" he asked, again telling me to sit. I thought I was dreaming? He said that he has been very harsh (harsh! I wanted to tell him that he had almost killed me!). "Well, don't worry. Next term you will be with me and we will enjoy flying together. Have a nice summer break." I just could not fathom this change! (The sad part is I did not get that opportunity to see his 'nice' side as he was soon posted out.)

During a function in the cadets' mess, I mentioned the sudden change in my instructor's behaviour towards me. To this, an army captain (from the Army, attending flying training) mentioned about the time when they (army officer and my instructor) were watching a hockey match between the Air Force Flying College and the Army. My instructor started to abuse me, asking how "that idiot Yadav can play so well?" The captain fired him and told him that he had exceeded all limits of bullying. "You have terrorised cadet Yadav, a boy who always has a smile on his face and knocked his smile off probably for life". I finally came to know why my instructor had changed. The rebuke probably chastened him. The Army captain was also his pupil and only survour, I was a miracle.

The rough patch in my flying training taught me a lesson which I carried for life, and was able to implement it on assuming command of the Selection Board. In my very first talk to the assessors, I advised then not to be bookish but go the extra mile with borderline cases, lest you lose a good person!

Postscript

Many years later I met my instructor (now a Wg. Cdr. Singhal) looking for the captain of the Super Constellation doing the Assam courier (who happened to be me). When I saw him, I ran to greet him. I guessed he was looking for a seat to go to the east. I took him straightaway to the relief crew compartment and made him comfortable. At Guwahati, I went to see him off where he gave me a longish hug and a warm handshake. I could see in his eyes that he was sorry for his rough behaviour. I returned the look, as if to say it was fine. I felt happy that I could be of some help. The fact is that he was my guru. I learnt how an eye or a look could convey so much, where words could not.

My Basic Stage and After

After I scraped through my basic stage, I remained a borderline case throughout inter and advance stages with no permanent instructor. The silver lining was that I was the star hockey player of the college. The aircraft during inter stage was the Taxon (T6G) (also known as the Harvard) and at the advance stage it was the Vampire.

The commandant (then Group Captain Radhkrishnen) and the Chief Ground Instructor were both were very fond of hockey. Therefore, hockey matches were frequent, particularly with the army.

Three flight cadets in the college team – Roach, Dias, and me. Whenever a match was arranged, the commandant's car would come to pick us up. On one occasion, the car, took us to the commandant's office. We wondered why?

There we learnt that an Under Officer flight cadet had reported us for not talking to the administration and our entire course was on punishment while the junior course was not. Roach was told to give up his sergeant cadet appointment.

Roach was thus reduced to an ordinary cadet. We were warned and punished by having to report to the guard room every hour during our free time.

Finally, I completed the course successfully and was commissioned as a pilot officer in the transport stream. Since our course had been trained on fighter aircraft, those of us slated for the transport stream were sent to Transport Training Wing (TTW) at Begumpet, Hyderabad.

We reported there for conversion training to Dakota (DC 3). Our stay at Hyderabad was uneventful except that in our group of eight, one had been a jockey. He introduced us to horse racing. The other activity was that we were regular visitors to the Secunderabad Club. Our favourite drink there was Napoleon Brandy with lime cordial.

WARRANT OFFICER UNIKRISHNAN: AIR FORCE FLYING COLLEGE, JODHPUR - 1960

The Air Force Flying College decided to present a PT display in honour of the AOC-in-C, Training Command, who was on an inspection visit.

The Chief Ground Instructor, Squadron Leader Dayal Singh detailed WO Unikrishnan to select, train and supervise the mass PT and gymnastics (horse) work.

He called all the ex-NDA flight cadets for gymnastics and the rest were asked to join the mass PT. I asked to be given a chance with the gymnastics team. He ignored my request. Generally, it is believed that

NDA cadets were superior to 'Direct Entry' (DE) cadets. To a certain extent, this might be true, but it is not a rule.

After the practice round was over and every one dispersed, I requested WO Unikrishnan to watch me perform on the horse and the ground exercises. He reluctantly agreed. I chose 'scissors' (considered to be a difficult exercise) and because it would not be performed by the gymnastics team. On ground work I just showed him 'fly spring'. He was impressed and took me into the gymnastics team.

I suggested that the last two for each items should be performed by the best cadets. He agreed. Flt. Cdt. Roach and I were selected for last two.

The mass PT and the horse work went of very well. I performed solo the 'fly spring', 'hand spring', 'head spring', 'front roll', 'and back roll' ending with a 'hand stand', dropping on the back and then getting up with a flip to face the AOC-in-C. The applause went on for almost a minute!

After the show, WO Unikrishnan said, "Cadet Yadav, did you notice the applause you received?" I told him he deserved the credit.

On one occasion, the CGI (then Sqn. Ldr. Dayal), decided to check the attendance at the morning PT. I was one of those bunking! All the absentees were given extra drill but I got away saying that I had taken permission from WO Unikrishnan. He confirmed it. I knew he liked me and that he would back me. (Later he did tell me that I should have told him before hand!)

On the eve of our course (79th pilot course) passing out, during the award giving ceremony, all the sports trophies were awarded to Flt. Cdt. Roach.

After the ceremony, Cadet Roach brought the trophies to me and said that they belonged to me. I told him that the college sees all angels before they come in any conclusion and that it really did not matter – we were both going to be pilot officers the next day. Let's enjoy our carrier in IAF.

Just before we were to leave for Hyderabad for our advance training, WO Unikrishnan knocked at my door.

My first reaction was to hope that all was well. The conversation went something like this: "Yes Sir, all well". "No, you don't have to call me 'Sir' – for you, I will always be Cadet Yadav."

Warrant Officer Unikrishnan was a perfect material as a GTI (Ground Training Instructor) for a training establishment. WO Krishnan you have come all the way to tell me that you had no role in selection of sports trophies awards, because he felt that trophies should have been awarded to me. I told WO Unikrishnan that the very fact you felt that way meant much more than those trophies, and I value your thoughts for me.

It's a pity that we never came across each other during our service carrier.

Thank you WO Unikrishnan you have always been my inspiration and motivation.

Chapter Six

Adventures in the Sky

ASHT-GRAHA: THE BEGINNINGS WITH THE SQUADRON – 1962 TO 1967

On 8 February 1962, the world was supposed to end

Asht-Graha was to occur from 4 to 8 February 1962, when eight celestial bodies – Sun, Moon, Earth, Mars, Venus, Saturn, Jupiter, and Mercury – would be aligned in a straight line. This phenomenon was supposed to magnify the effect of gravity and impact some geographical factors directly affecting the Earth. The planet was waiting for *pralay* (doomsday).

It was a coincidence that whilst the *Asht-Graha* fever was on, eight pilot officers were posted on 5 February 1962 to No. 12 Squadron at Agra. These eight came to be known throughout the station as '*Asht-Graha*' because of the astrological prediction.

All of us were accommodated in No. 2 Officers' Mess. The senior-most officers in this mess were the two PJIs (Para Jump Instructors), both known to be holy terrors. All new arrivals had to call on them. However, all went well and we were adopted as the *Asht-Graha* 8 – Pilot Officers V.K. Sharma, S.S. Chopra, M. Ferdinand, C.R. Ghosh, V.S. Yadav, G.S. Brar, A.K. Patro, and Agnihotri.

We acquired bicycles to go to the Squadron. First thing in the morning was to attend the Met Briefing in O I/C Flying Complex. Since the Met Briefing was early in the morning, our bearer would bring bread and omelette packed in a newspaper and fix it on the cycles. When we came

Transport stream my course mates
1st Row, left to right: Sharma, Ferdinand, Pathania, Agnihotri, Yadav and Patro
2nd Row, left to right: Hardial, Sahota, Brar, Chopra, Ranganath and Ghosh

out after the briefing, we found that crows had feasted on our breakfast! So the first lesson we learned was to protect it. After reporting to the Squadron, we were told to inform our arrival report to all sections of the station, and familiarise ourselves with their location and functions.

Next, we acquired a motor cycle (Indian) and a scooter to move around – five on the motor cycle and three on the scooter. We explored Agra in this manner. Sadar Bazar in the cantonment was popular and patronised mostly by army and air force officers; the only good restaurant was Kwality.

We became regular visitors to Kwality restaurant. They served good food and our usual order was *tandoori* chicken, brain curry with *tandoori roti*, followed by coffee with cream. By then we started to be known as 'five on a motor cycle and three on scooter.'

Once, we decided to invite some of our married seniors for dinner at the restaurant. We had a music system (in those days it was Ahuja) that we took with us and created a little dance floor. It went off so well that we started repeating this activity until it became a regular musical evening. The restaurant started becoming popular.Our next exploration of Agra was a cinema hall in *Kinari Bazar*, where the movie *Junglee* was running.

We saw it 17 times and the local population got used to seeing us as five on a motor cycle and three on scooter.

Settling In

Frequent late nights became routine, and as only one of us went to the Squadron in the mornings we were not really missed. After a month or so, the Flight Commander suddenly noticed the absentees. He asked the one present where the others were. When told that they were on arrival report, he ordered all the eight to be in the Squadron within half an hour. Our 'rep' rushed back to the officers' mess and woke us up. We were all present in the Squadron, and were told that our training would commence the following week.

Raju had been No. 1 (head waiter) with No. 2 Officers' Mess for over a decade. All those from Packet and Canberra Squadrons who have gone through Agra will never forget him. He is a legend.

Though there are strict timings for mess meals, Raju never allowed anyone to go hungry. We, the *Asht-Graha* 8 were adopted by Raju instantly. I remember one Sunday morning, an outstation aircrew was having breakfast and I heard them asking Raju how come they were having chicken curry, etc., at the other table. Raju told them that they were having their dinner! Raju would at times play pranks on us. Once he gave us finger bowls with boiling hot water. When we gave him an inquiring look, he replied, "Sorry Sir, I cannot give hotter than this".

That was Raju. He will always remain in our hearts.

After we qualified as co-pilots, three of us – Sharma, Chopra, and Ferdinand – were transferred to the Squadron in Srinagar.

Inter-unit sports also took place. Our Navigator course mates who reported to the Squadron six months earlier told the sports officer that I had been a good sportsman at the academy. I was invited to participate in the strategy sessions to try to win the inter-unit trophy. After knowing all the sports personnel of the Squadron, I reorganised the football, hockey, and athletic teams.

I remained in the sports field from morning till evening – organising, training, and motivating. That resulted in our winning the cup.

I participated fully in football and hockey, but in athletics took part only in the long jump. One day I called a young pilot officer to be on time for his event. I told him that as I had been there the whole day, I would rest a bit before my event in the afternoon; the young pilot did not turn up and we lost that event. It so happened that the CO landed up and found that our participant was missing. When I arrived he was so angry that he almost took my pants off. I was heartbroken. The CO didn't even know whose hard work had won us the cup.

After a few months, the remaining five were also attached to the Squadron in Srinagar and so all eight again got together. Our activities in Srinagar started. We discovered two restaurants – Capri and Premier – that were patronised mainly during the summer season. The owner of Capri was a friend of our CO and we were thus allowed to sign instead of paying cash.

Whenever there was any activity in Srinagar we eight were there, whether in the two restaurants or at Dal Lake for shikara rides, or at Nagin Lake for water skiing or Amar Singh Club for Tambola.

On one occasion a troupe from Bombay came to perform at Capri. In our presence, the crooner passed a derogatory remark on the Air Force. Patro, who was a little sensitive, told the crooner to take his words back but the latter refused. Patro would have actually beaten him but for our CO who happened to be there and told us to leave.

On another occasion, at the Premier restaurant on the eve of Independence Day, we asked the restaurant band to play the National Anthem. They refused; the management also refused to serve any more drinks. Just then my cousin, Col. Ram Singh (who was commanding the Winter Warfare School at Gulmarg) arrived with his officers and told the owner, get the band to play the National Anthem. They jolly well played it.

My cousin invited us to Gulmarg where he treated us as his own officers.

When 19 Squadron moved to Agra and 12 Squadron to Srinagar, three of our course mates moved to Agra while five continued with our Squadron. In winter we moved to Pathankot.

In 1965 we were scrambled to Bareilly, and operated from there. I remember during winter there used to be thick fog and aircraft could not take off till it lifted. On many occasions the fog would remain till late afternoon thereby it would be too late to proceed to the forward area. So a course mate (Dada Ghosh) and I found a way. At AF Station Bareilly, working hours were from 7:30 in morning to 1:30 in the afternoon; from then to 7:30 the next morning, a duty officer handled all the activities of the station including Air Traffic Control. As the duty officer would always be from our Squadron, we started to schedule our take off before 7 in the morning saying that in case of an emergency we would divert to either Agra or Palam. So normally there were two aircraft always airborne.

Finally, the Squadron moved to Pathankot. On two occasions during my flight to Thoise airfield, the aircraft would back fire on the take-off run but clear before the lift off speed. Once, a captain, who was to take-off behind me, called out to reject take-off as the engines were back firing. However, I continued and the back fire stopped.

I remember once the same aircraft back fire happened at Pathankot, so I retuned to have it checked. Just then our CO landed from Agra and wanted to know why the aircraft had returned. There had been occasions where one particular officer would often cancel flights claiming loss of power. When that happened more than a few times, the CO thought he was shamming and took him for a power check where the aircraft was found to be fine. Similarly, the CO thought I was shamming and did not want to do the second sortie. He decided to take me for a power check. When we taxied to the runway the aircraft started back firing so loudly that the ATC told us to switch off! The aircraft was an IK 462 and I can never forget that incident. The fact is the entire Squadron knew that there are two guys crazy about flying; if one of them took off, you could be rest assured the other would, even if the engine failed, I was one of the two. Unfortunately, the CO was not aware of this fact. A great lesson for me; you must know your men whom you command.

I made a vow that if I ever command a Squadron, I would make sure I know each and every person serving in it.

AHMED KHEL DAY

After the *Asht-Graha* fever was over, I decided to take a few days off to spend time with my eldest brother, then posted at Gurdaspur (Punjab). Reaching there, I realised that he had moved from 2/3 GR to 4/3 GR, a newly raised battalion. With its first CO Lt. Col. R.K. Duleep Singh raised at Dehradun.

It also coincided with celebration of Ahmed Khel Day, which is celebrated to commemorate the gallant action of their forebears, the 3rd Gurkhas.

The battle of Ahmed Khel took place during the second Anglo-Afghan War on 19 April 1880 between Afghan tribesmen and the British Indian Army in which the 3rd Gurkhas took active part. Ahmed Khel is a village 30 miles from Ghazni on the road from Kandahar to Kabul.

The usual celebration is a Pagal Gymkhana with various stalls and a football match between officers and JCOs. I remember the CO's wife taking all the newly posted bachelor officers to all the stalls. There was stall in which a rope ladder led to a bottle of beer. Mrs. Duleep asked the young officers to try and get the beer. No one succeeded. Mrs. Duleep asked me to try. I knew the only way to climb was not to use the 'steps' but push up using the first class rope climb technique. I not only got the bottle of beer but also appreciation. Retired veterans of the battalion who were present wanted to know when this new subaltern had joined the regiment. I was then introduced as the IAF subaltern of the 4/3 Gorkha Rifles.

I also participated in their football match. The unique thing about it was that the officer's team had set up a bar at their goal and similarly the JCOs had one at theirs. On any team scoring a goal, the captain of the opposing team invited the goal scoring team to their bar to have one large rum in one gulp and the game resumed. It is great fun to watch the game at the closing stages!

All officers participated in games in the late afternoon and the ladies either went swimming or played badminton.

Lt. Chanda, who was the senior most among the bachelor officers, invited me for drinks in the Officers' Mess. It was only a few metres from my brother's accommodation. Predictably, the evening stretched on! My *Bhabhi* (sister-in-law) sent my brother to fetch me, fearing that I might have drunk too much. My brother did come but also joined the drinking session. We returned to the house pretty late. Though I was able to walk back, my condition was bad. (This was evident as my *Bhabhi* told me later that while I was trying to eat, I could barely find my mouth!).

Before leaving for Agra I thanks CO Col. Daleep and his wife for adopting me into 4/3 GR and gifted me with a GORKHA HAT.

I often visited 4/3 GR, particularly during their Dussehra functions which they celebrate with great *josh* and gusto.

Many years later when 4/3 GR was located in Leh (Ladakh) and I was flying Packet aircraft, their men who were passengers would tell the crew and other passengers that I was part of them and the aircraft too!

The 3rd Gurkha Rifles

It is my proud privilege to mention that our family has been part of legacy of 3 GR and each member of our family has represented all its battalions.

My younger brother, Col. Aman Yadav, served in 1/3 GR. My eldest brother, Maj. Gen. S.D.S. Yadav of 2/3 GR, later 4/3, my *tauji's* son, Col. Ram Singh (my cousin) of 3/3 GR. my eldest brother's son, Lt. Gen. Karan Yadav (my nephew) of 4/3 GR, my eldest brother and his son commanded the 4/3 GR and I was adopted as the Air Force Subaltern of 4/3 GR.

It may probably be the reason why the 3rd Gurkha Rifles preferred Maj. Gen. S.D.S. Yadav (my eldest brother) to be their Colonel of the Regiment.

PICTORIAL

First day at Sanawar Feb 1951

Chora becomes Gentlemen

With DQ, Dr. Purewal and Maj Vijay Ratan Choudhary MVC at Sanawar 1953

DADA GHOSH.
Batchmate flying together

After Commisioning with IAF pilot officer

Final Stage Vampire 1961 Judhpur

Trek to Mt. Chor Simla Hills 1954

Sanawar Soccer Team 1954

WE SIX. Sanawar 1954

Recieving Trophy

My marriage May 1967

My two boys

At Fukshe Ladhak 1964

Dr Gurudev Purewal stint to become Filmstar

My elder sister and her family

Rao Lal Singh leading the barat, my marriage

Thank you IAF. Last day in office 1993

With Air Chief after President color

SQN visitor book signing by President with CAS two C-n-C and self

My Nephew Lt Gen Karan recieving PVSM

Air Chief Indonesia after his son met an air accident

My Yonger brother Col. Aman explaining President Dr. Rajender Prasad at NDA

With King of Bhutan after Taj

We 4 brothers fought 62, 65 & 71 wars

My flight to Fukshr Ladhak

Defence Minister Jagjeewan Ram

SQN Re-Union Recieving Guest

Sqn Cake Re-Union

Sqd. Re-union. My wife with C-n-C wife Mrs. Green

My wife seeing off the Air Chief's wife Sunita Mehra

Tanvir Ahmed Chaudhry DIG at palatial house at Lahore with me and my wife

Final Bye-bye to the Uniform

At Gujranwala Pakistan. Recieved at Gargoli Lawrence college

Golf Tournamnet Dehradun. ACM Dilbagh Singh Ex-IAF Chief Gen Bakshi with the team

'We won Kargil with ingenuity'

THE ASIAN AGE 6 OCTOBER 1999

My Son Gp. Capt Monish after Kargil

My Tauji after WW1. All JCO's of 2/19 Hyderabad with Battalion Cmd Maj Rackette

My Father after 1918

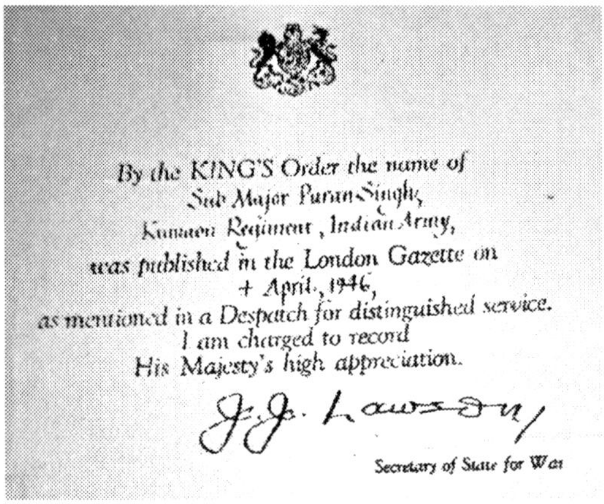

By the KING'S Order the name of
Sub Major Puran Singh,
Kumaon Regiment, Indian Army,
was published in the London Gazette on
4 April, 1946,
as mentioned in a Despatch for distinguished service.
I am charged to record
His Majesty's high appreciation.

J.J. Lawson

Secretary of State for War

My fathers mention-in-dispatch (WWII)

Two elder brothers. Heros of 71 war

My Tauji Capt. Hari Singh Coronation King George VI

Anirudh with his father and his father-in-law

My Sister

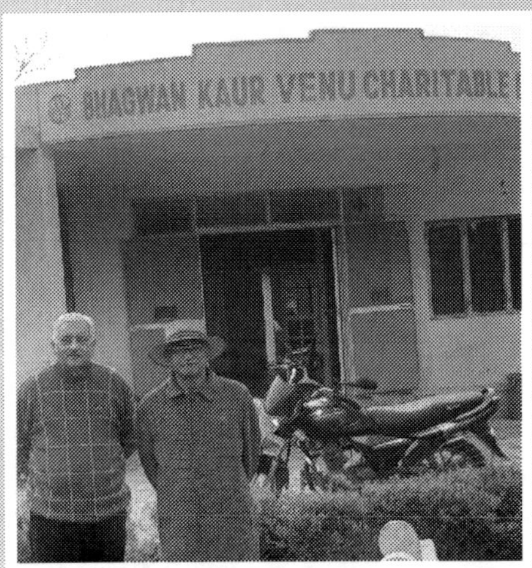

My nephew at our village charitable hospital

Ms Tanuja Joshi MD, Venu eye institute, Chief Guest

Rhea and her father

Shreya with her father

Shri Morarji Desai after the Jorat crash

My two sons at golf

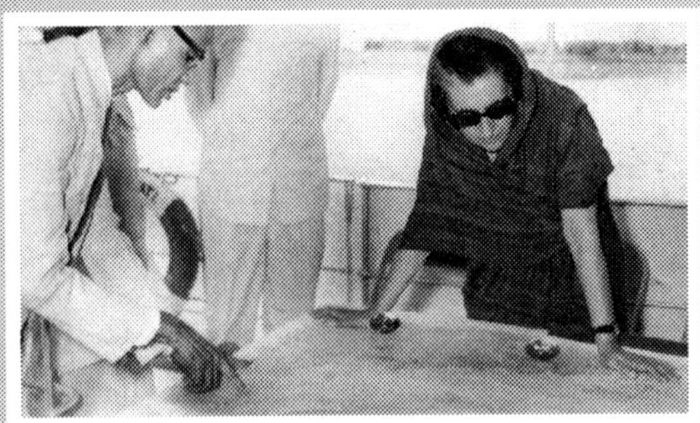

My father-in-law briefs Prime Minister Smt Indira Gandhi

Two sons, senior commanders at Indigo

Packet cockpit

My wife and son recieving me after London air miss

ASHT-GRAHA DAYS
A ROMANCE THAT FAILED

In 1965, I met a girl at a wedding. She came up to me and we exchanged pleasantries. She was in class XII. I noticed that she would find some excuse or the other to converse with me. I, on the other hand, found her to be a charming person. That she would speak with confidence meant she probably came from a good home. After the wedding was over, she came up to me and asked if she could write to me. I started liking her. I remember in school I was a big sports star and thought myself to be a big stud, but when it came to girls, they had their own idea. I had liked a girl at school but she preferred a boy who was neither good in games nor in studies. I thought he was rather girlish. I developed a complex that no girl would ever like me. So when this girl wanting to be friend, I was surprised. I asked her why she wanted to write to me, but her answer simply was that she liked me.

The correspondence soon became a daily affair and then I began visiting her. The Squadron had moved to Agra from Srinagar/Pathankot. Whenever there was a flight to Palam in Delhi with a night halt there, I would volunteer. By then everyone in the Squadron was aware of my 'interest'. I was lucky that the Squadron was tasked to do 'Yankee' courier which originated from Agra on a Tuesday via Delhi and returned on Friday. I would then take three day's leave, scrounge a lift and then head for her place.

She knew my routine and invariably waited for me every Tuesday. Accommodation was never a problem – Club/Army Officers' Mess. Even if there was a flight with a night halt at Palam I always managed to meet her, and the crew would be keen to help.

Our love and affection deepened. We started to crave for each other's company. Thoughts of marriage bloomed. I told my parents about her and her community. They were initially hesitant, but relented once they learnt that she was from army background. My parents requested my eldest brother and my *Bhabhi* to meet her. They approved of her, finding her charming and affectionate.

The girl was certain that her parents would never agree as they were highly caste conscious and, therefore, she suggested a court marriage. Even though we did meet a lawyer (against my wishes), we did not proceed because I always felt that parental blessings are a must for any successful marriage. I then told her that as both families belong to a defence background, I was confident her parents would agree. Normally defence personnel are generally above caste.

On one of my trips to her, I saw her father standing outside the house. I paid my compliments and wished him, but he was quite rude and told me that his daughter had decided to have nothing to do with me and that I should not write or try to meet her. He asked me to return all her letters. I told him I would like to hear from her directly.

She echoed what her father had said. I told her I will return all that her father wanted. In the end, I said "I wish to say, you have been a great girl. I wish you all happiness for the future. And finally, as there is prodigious strength in sorrow and despair, for you and any one dear to you, I would do anything GOOD BYE."

On my way back, I kept wondering what kind of destiny God had laid out for me? He makes me feel I am no good, then he tells me I am a great sports person, allows me to fail and then tells me that failures are good for you.

During my failed courtship, I had often talked about my mother. I told her that after marriage, she would take care of her and always be with us.

Thoroughly disappointed at the turn of events, I decided never to marry and devote my life to looking after my mother.

Eventually I did get married and my wife promised that she will take care of my mother the way I wished to.

ASHT-GRAHA DAYS
SRINAGAR/PATHANKOT

The Routine at Srinagar

All the aircraft had returned from their second sortie to the Ladakh airfields;, it was around 3 p.m. Reaching the accommodation at Gupkar Road took about an hour. A quick lunch and off to sleep. Shaving and bathing 9:30 or 10 p.m., we would hit the bar. Barman Amir knew everyone's drink. Gossiping about Kashmiri girls, discussing interesting incidents of the sortie, and envying the married guys went on till past midnight. We could snatch an hour's sleep before catching the morning transport at 4 a.m. Met briefing at 5 a.m., our eyes still half closed. Back to the Squadron to pick up our parachutes and then head for our aircraft. Take offs were permitted only at dawn or half an hour before sunrise. The Packet (C119G) is a piston engine aircraft, unpressurised and its full throttle height is around 6,000 feet. Therefore, to operate the airfields in Ladakh, we needed to engage superchargers. The superchargers were engaged only if the aircraft was to be flown at higher altitudes and not as a rule. However, since we were operating in Ladakh, we needed to climb up to 21,000 feet and engaging the superchargers had become routine. We had to wear oxygen masks which were a bit uncomfortable. (So we resorted to Hukka, taking oxygen direct fix on the pipe.)

Over the mountains we could see the sun rising from the snow covered mountains – a sight so phenomenally beautiful, it was just marvellous.

At each destination be it Leh, Thoise, Chushul or Fukshe, we were received warmly, with a nice mug of tea. By the time we finished our tea the aircraft was off loaded.

On one occasion after landing at Thoise, the weather went bad and we were stranded for three days just in overalls. On the third day the weather cleared and we took off to return to base. Just after take-off, we experienced a partial loss of power one engine. Since we had a third engine (an extra Jet pack one), we decided to continue, but we had to do orbits to get out of the Thoise valley. When we neared Kargil, we saw bad weather approaching from the west. So we attempted to take an alternate route but could not manage it. We decided to divert and as we turned towards Leh, the weather started moving so fast that we were able to clear the ridge just in the nick of time. Then we noticed the fuel warning, so we switched off the jet pack to save fuel, hoping to make it safely to Leh. Packet aircraft take-offs and landings were on runway 25 but landing was allowed on 07 only an emergency. I informed the ATC that I was short of fuel and would be landing on runway 07. We landed and had just reached the parking area when our fuel finished. It was a close call indeed!.

We operated 24/7, round the year. Stand down occurred only if the weather was bad. The day stand down was declared, the whole Squadron was out to either on the Dal Lake for *shikara* rides or Nagin Lake for water skiing.

Pathankot

The only difference at Pathankot was that we stayed at the airfield itself in tents. As it took about 15 minutes only to the Met Briefing, we get almost an extra hour to sleep!

Asht-Graha Days
My Mother Suffers a Paralytic Attack

The Squadron, even the new CO, learnt about my break up. They sympathised with me. Now on my trips to Delhi I would invariably request Delhi ATC for a practice hold over Pataudi Beacon (PTD) at low height. As in those days there was not much air traffic at Delhi Airport, ATC would always agree. The holding pattern was over my elder sister's house so she would know that I would be visiting her and therefore make my favourite special *halwa* ready. After my mother, it was my sister that I was very attached to. Many years later, after I retired, I was unable to meet my sister regularly due to my frequent visits to Dehradun where I was building a house. But, when I learnt that she was admitted in a hospital at Gurgaon, I rushed to meet her. On seeing me her first reaction was, *'Bhai aap ki baat dekhte dekhte mair layi'* (*Bhai*, I nearly died waiting for you). She died a few years later and her passing away was as much a loss to me as my mother's demise. On one such visit, I was stopped on the way by my brother-in-law. He informed me that my mother had suffered a paralytic attack. We headed for Safdarjung Hospital where my mother was admitted. After the break-up, she had decided to visit me at Agra. Normally she did not travel. She was accompanied by my elder sister and her husband. I put them up in Agra Club. I tried to put up brave front, but as the saying goes – one can fool everyone, but not their mother.

On her return she took a break at my sister's place as it was a long journey to reach our village. While there, she refused to eat or even drink water as it was the tradition to do so at one's daughter's place. Knowing that my mother is very serious about rituals, I should have known that my mother will not eat or drink even water at her daughter's place. I did not know this. When I did come to know, I cursed myself. The least I could have done was to have food packed for her. This could have prevented the dehydration that led to her paralytic attack.

We had rented a house near Safdarjung Hospital in Green Park so that the family could attend to my mother. As the house was unfurnished, I contacted the contractor who had provided furniture for the rooms of No. 2 Officers' Mess where I was staying. When I mentioned about my mother, he made available all the furniture we needed. I was able to ferry it in on my next trip to Palam. With help from an old school friend, now an army officer also posted at Agra, I could arrange a vehicle to the rented house. During my frequent visits to Delhi, my friend Col. Harinder Mankotia, would also try and accompany me to visit my mother.

I am really grateful to Sqn. Ldr. Prabhakar from the Air II Branch WAC who had helped me with night halts at Palam during my visits to Meerut and now allowed me to stay at Palam whenever operating for commitment in J&K.

My Wedding
Muh Dekhayi

After the wedding at Mussoorie we returned to our village Sadat Nagar. All the rituals/ceremonies were being done to welcome and receive the bride (my wife Renu), one such ceremony was Muh Dekhayi.

Muh Dekhayi is basically to introduce the newly wed bride to all the ladies of close relations and the village women, in return all the ladies then gift the bride as NEG either in form of cash or kind (item) I do remember some of remark the ladies made 'chhori tho sohni se aur gori bhee' (the girl is good looking and fair complexion.)

Many years later after retirement during my visits to my elder sister who would often talk about my childhood tantrums, on one such visit mentioned how my mother remained away from the Muh Dekhayi ceremony of my wife when she came home in the village as a bride. My mother then had just recovered from her paralytic attack after a year in bed. By then my mother possessed nothing or wore no jewellery, even the last piece of jewellery the CHAIN which she was very possessive of was also sold off. My sister told me that time it just did not occur that mother may not have anything to give to the bride.

Knowing my mother how serious she has been with rituals must have gone through trauma for not being part of the MUH DEKHAYI, I felt awfully bad. I had mentioned to my father that be lavish with all the Negs for which I had contributed.

The best I could do under the circumstance was I requested Kanjimul and Sons (jewellers) to make a gold Chain exactly the same design my mother used to wear, her most precious jewellery. (As it was gift from her Nani)

I then told my wife that my mother owed you something when you came as a bride for Muh Dekhayi, which she was unable to give you then, so please accept this CHAIN on her behalf, which is replica of the Chain my mother's most valued piece of jewellery.

Though my wife did not remember that mother was not part of the Muh Dekhayi ceremony, but this Chain had become valued remembrance.

My Marriage

On one of the visits to see my mother, Harinder was with me. She told him, 'Bhai Harinder, please get this son of mine married, as he will die but will never ask for anything for himself'. When I looked at her, I could really feel that even her *atma* (soul) was under severe stress. Harinder too felt the same and assured my mother that he would do something.

Col. Harinder was staying in the same Officers' Mess as Col. Harsh Yadav (brother of my younger brother's wife). He learnt that Harsh was looking for a match for his cousin who was studying in Bombay's Sophia College. On one of my trips there, Harinder decided to accompany me and forced me to visit the college to meet the cousin, Renu. After meeting her, he told Col. Harsh to propose the marriage to my parents. They gladly accepted.

I was sent on a course to Coimbatore from November 1966 to January 1967. Before proceeding, Harinder and I went to see my mother. She told our family members that the engagement ceremony was to be done even if I was not present.

After I returned from the course at Coimbatore, good things started to happen. My marriage was fixed for 19 May 1967. My mother recovered and my posting to Pune to No. 6 Squadron (considered to be an elite one) came through. Pune is one of the best air force stations, particularly for married officers.

Renu and I were welcomed with a lot of fanfare by my new Squadron. We also learnt that eight new couples had joined the Squadron in the same month.

A new chapter of my life as a newly married officer was to begin with a new Squadron.

Chapter Seven

VIP Squadron Years (1974–82)

No. 6 Squadron, AF Station, Pune 1967 to 1974

Pune marked a new chapter in my life. I would fly better aircraft, at a better station and also begin a new life as a family man.

My wife, Renu, was from a civilian background though her cousins were in the defence services. She had been brought up in Kandla (Gujarat) where her father was with the Kandla Port Trust. So we both were in a new environment.

We reached Pune with just personal belongings and stayed in the house of someone who was on leave. (I was waiting to be allotted accommodation.) The house had only beds with linen and the kitchen had a stove and a few utensils. I remember our first meal with no crockery or cutlery so we ate with our hands directly from the utensils! That was the first meal of our married life at Pune – most enjoyable and memorable. It remains the best meal we ever had. Renu pointed out that there were no curtains, so off I went to one of our bachelor colleague's room and took his curtains. And that is how we started together and built a home – bit by bit, brick by brick. (I learnt later that my wife had never accepted any gifts from her parents but had told them the best gift they could give was to always respect her husband and her in-laws.)

Pune (then Poona) was a great city and the Air Force station, even better. Since the Squadron was undertaking courier to UK, it was big attraction. During that year the Squadron saw eight more weddings so there were parties almost daily for the newlyweds.

My training on the Super Constellation aircraft was slow, but I was enjoying married life fully. During this period, I was promoted to the rank of Squadron Leader and we were blessed with two sons – my elder son was delivered by Dr. Koyaji, considered to be the best gynaecologist in Bombay region and my younger son at Command Hospital, Pune.

Renu, though married when only a few months over eighteen, was very mature. Her life revolved around her two boys, her husband and her home with complete dedication and discipline. She set up our home with whatever resources we had to a very comfortable level. Even now at the age of 75, her focus is on her sons, grandchildren, and their well-being.

After having qualified on Super Constellations, my first trip as co-pilot was a hair raising experience. Near misses over London, first with a hill on the approach to the Royal Airbase Northolt and later with a Boeing 727 of Columbia Airways. It was really a miracle to have survived. (The details of this flight are enumerated separately.)

After my satisfying tenure and my good performance acknowledged by AEB, I was posted to Air HQ Communication Squadron (the VIP Squadron), considered to be the most sought after transport squadron.

No. 6 Maritime Squadron: A Legacy in Vigilance

The primary role of No. 6 Maritime Squadron was maritime search and rescue, surveillance of hostile elements across the Indian Ocean and Bay of Bengal, and routine transport operations. After my posting in May 1967, I was detailed to undergo a Maritime Course with the Indian Navy at Naval Base Cochin. Interestingly, at the end of each lecture, instructors consistently emphasised that the Maritime Squadron should belong to the Navy. Even during the closing address, the Naval Base Commander reiterated the Navy's desire to absorb the Squadron.

Years later, on 20 November 1973, while on a UK courier mission, I landed at RAF St. Mawgan to pick up a consignment for the IAF. During our stay, we interacted with RAF officers from their Maritime Squadron.

When asked if the Royal Navy had ever tried to claim their squadron, their response was unanimous and proud: they were RAF through and through.

This sentiment was reflected across the UK. In various parts of London, including near London Bridge, I came across memorials bearing Prime Minister Winston Churchill's immortal words from the Battle of Britain:

> *"Never in the field of human conflict was so much owed by so many to so few."*

Such tributes underscore the deep national pride and emotional connection the British people have with the RAF. A rumour circulated in our crew room back then – that the Royal Navy once attempted to claim RAF Maritime Squadrons in the British Parliament. A senior MP was reported to have responded that, considering the RAF's legacy and sacrifices, such a move would have a profoundly negative impact on morale. The house, reportedly, agreed that the squadrons would remain with the RAF. (This account was never officially confirmed – it remained part of the crew room folklore.)

In contrast, the Indian Air Force did eventually lose its Maritime Squadron to the Indian Navy. Yet, No. 6 Squadron had earned an enviable reputation:

> *"You could throw a cigarette butt into the Indian Ocean and they'd find it."*

We were trained to identify any warship – its class, its nationality, its combat role – with precision. That legacy of excellence in maritime reconnaissance remains a source of immense pride.

Morale remains one of the most enduring principles of war.

LIBERATOR B-24, GIFT TO CANADA

The Canadian Government requested Air HQ through the Indian Government if a Liberator Aircraft (B-24) from No. 6 Squadron could be gifted to Canada for their War Museum. The Government of India graciously agreed. The Liberator, one of the iconic bomber aircraft of the Second World War, was extensively used for bombing Berlin (among other German cities).

The Canadian High Commissioner deputed the Canadian Military Attaché, Col. Pudsey, to co-ordinate with the IAF. The Canadian ferry aircrew brought their own communications system and liquor to give a befitting party to No. 6 Squadron!

At a speech to celebrate the transfer of the Liberator, Col. Pudsey said, "After the decision to hand over one of the Liberators to Canada was taken, I was invited by the Indian Air Chief to his house for dinner. Because of the spicy food, I needed to visit the loo. After use, I pulled the chain a number of times to flush but the water tank of the commode (WC) did not work. This was most embarrassing, to say the least. Later when I arrived in Pune, the AOC called me for dinner. Once again I found the food too spicy, and had to visit the loo. I pulled the chain and again the flush did not work! The next day I was invited to a meal by CO 6 Squadron, and the Indian food was spicy again. After the inevitable visit to the loo, to my surprise the commode flush once again did not work! It was all too embarrassing. I then wondered if the chain of the flush system worked only for Indians. I therefore brought a Canadian commode, which only a Canadian can operate (this was a replica of the Indian wooden commode) and requested the CO, Gp. Capt. J.B. Lall, to pull the chain. It did not work! I then asked the AOC, then Air Cmde. Idris Latif to pull the chain and it still did not work!"

Then Col. Pudsey showed that the commode would work only if operated by a Canadian. He pulled the chain, the sound of a commode flushing came and it worked! He poured the liquid that came out to the AOC and said, "Sir, have a drink". It was whisky! Very cleverly, a bottle of whisky had been set as a 'water tank' and the chain fitted to a peg measure!

This beautiful gift became part of No. 6 Squadron's valuable collection of memorabilia (see photo).

Near Collision at Northolt RAF Base, UK (9 January 1970)

A major incident happened with a No. 6 Squadron aircraft over London in 1970. I was the co-pilot of the aircraft. I am detailing here an analysis of the incident based on the investigation carried out by Mr. W.H. Tench of the Investigating Branch of the Department of Trade and Industries, Strand, London, detailing the circumstances leading to a near collision firstly with the hill on approach to Runway 26 of Northolt by the IAF Super Constellation (registration BG579) and subsequently with a Boeing 727 of Olympic Airways (registration SXCBB) on 9 January 1970. I am providing further details of the incident as also my recollection of all that went on inside the cockpit, since we did not have a voice recorder in the aircraft. To put the incident in context, the reader may like to know the weather conditions (WX) over Northolt, London that day:

Surface Winds	190/16 knots	
Weather	Light Rain	
Visibility	5 km	
Clouds	4/8 Stratus Ht 1100′	
	5/8 Strato-cumulus	Ht 1300′
	4/8 Strato-cumulus	Ht 1600′
QNH	996.3 millibars	
QFE	991.7 millibars	

I will start from NDB Epsom. After reporting over Epsom, we were handed over by Military Radar to Northolt Radar. After establishing contact with it, we were given a course to steer. We were to descend to 1,250 feet and maintain on QFE for a straight-in approach to Northolt Runway 26. When the captain continued to descend below 1,250 feet despite instructions not to, he was cautioned by both the Navigator (who was handling communications) and I not to descend further. However, he continued to maintain the descent profile. Northolt Radar warned on every R/T call not to descend and to maintain 1,250 feet. We continued to descend against the advice of the radar controller.

Realising that we were not reacting to his calls and finding us well below the glide slope, Northolt Radar called to say that he had lost us on the screen and requested our height. We reported we were at 500 feet. The next call from Radar was, "If you read me, hill two miles ahead of you, height 637 feet. Climb immediately to 1,500 feet and turn left".

The captain did not react to this call too. It took me about 15-20 seconds to realise there was a hill in front of us and we not only were below it but heading straight for it. By then we were at 400 feet. I shouted to the flight engineer for take-off power and yanked back the controls as harshly as I could, though I did not initiate the left turn. For the next one and half to two minutes there was total silence.

The Radar Controller later mentioned that in those 90 seconds he was 500 per cent certain that we had crashed. He also mentioned seeing an aircraft heading for the hill and found himself helpless in averting a disaster. He said he could not believe our call after 90 seconds that we were at 1,500 feet and turning left. He was in such shock to hear from us that it took him 15 seconds to acknowledge the call.

A few important points need to be mentioned here before proceeding further. Firstly, why did the Radar Controller asked us to turn left, knowing that it would interfere with the safety lane of Runway 23 of Heathrow? The reason given later was that since we were well below the hill and not answering his calls, he felt that the only chance we had of survival was to turn left as only the left edge of the hill was in line with Runway 26 and the major part of the hill was to the right. Hence, he thought that a right turn would entail clearing the hill, given how low we were. However, if we had turned left immediately on his command and not after about 90 seconds as we did, in all probability we would have been well clear of the Boeing 727 for Heathrow.

On my part, I only yanked the stick back and did not actually take over the controls. Even for the left turn I had to tell the captain to please turn left. I must mention here even if there was delay of just seven seconds in my pulling back the stick there was no way that we could have avoided crashing into the hill.

The Board of Inquiry re-constructed the flight with a C-130 Hercules and found that I initiated the climb 23 seconds after the call was given by the radar controller and cleared the hill by just 77 feet. If you worked it out mathematically, it was observed that if there had been a delay of just seven seconds, even with a max rate of climb we would never have been be able to clear the hill.

In a statement by an eye-witness living on the hill to BBC News, the man said he felt that the aircraft was going to enter his balcony and that we had missed his house by inches.

In the subsequent approaches made by the captain, he started to descend well before we were cleared to descend. On my part, knowing now that there was a hill at approach height 637 feet, I did not allow him to descend below 800 feet. It is at this stage I realised that the captain was finding it difficult to make an approach even after three unsuccessful attempts. I, in fact, carried out the last approach – all I did was just follow the instructions given and maintained the course and height given by the Radar Controller. I was over-riding the controls from the captain and started the descent only after we were cleared to do so. The Radar Controller realised that there was some kind of a panic in the cockpit and started to give us confidence by saying that the approach was very good, that we are on the glide slope and on the centre line. Finally, we both, or rather I, landed the aircraft.

Before I try and give my analysis for why the captain behaved in the manner he did, I need to make a confession. During the pre-flight briefing by the CO, he had mentioned that since the captain has been on the courier and to Northolt several times, there was nothing more to be added. As for the co-pilot, he said since this was my first time to the UK I should just enjoy myself. On my part, I took that briefing literally and did not prepare or try to find out anything regarding the route, arrival/ departure procedures or the terminal approach procedures. This resulted in my total ignorance that there was a hill on the approach for Runway 26 Northolt. I had no idea that the missed approach for Runway 26 is to the north, that is right turn and left turn is prohibited, as it would interfere with the Heathrow airport. I must admit that had I prepared and updated myself as I was expected to do as a crew member, this embarrassing situation could have been avoided.

I personally feel it all started at Paris when we were to leave for the airport from the hotel. One of our crew members got talking to some people staying in the same hotel and they realised that we were 13 people on board and that it was a Friday! They commented that it was very unlucky; it so happened that as we taxied out we had a brake problem. After a delay of more than four hours, the brakes could not be repaired. However, the local engineer confirmed that out of eight brake assemblies on four wheels, even if one was disconnected the braking effect would be as good. We then took off for Northolt.

I remember during the entire flight the captain was very quiet and never spoke a word. The only thing he uttered as if to himself – a few times in Punjabi – was that Northolt Runway is short and that we have a brake problem. On hearing this, I did tell him that our seven brake assemblies are working so there should be no problem at all. I think in his sub-conscious mind it got registered that we were 13 on board, on a Friday and that we have a brake problem; the runway is short and it would be a night landing, which he had never done before. With all this on his mind, he became so stressed that no inputs, either from the crew or the radar controller would register. He was so quiet and focussed on his own thoughts that we as crew members found it very difficult to convey anything.

I found myself in a very difficult situation. This was my first international flight and the captain was my instructor. He had been to Northolt several times so my taking over the controls would be very unusual. Under the circumstances, I must say that the Radar Controller, Flg. Offr. M.J. Eaton may be given full credit for saving the aircraft and our lives from a catastrophic disaster. If he had not mentioned that there was a hill in front of us, there was no way I would have reacted and climbed steeply, thereby avoiding a collision.

In the end, I must admit that it was an inexcusable display of professional incompetence – total ignorance of terminal approach procedures and lack of detailed knowledge of general surroundings.

Took over Controls Unofficially

After the fourth unsuccessful approach (each approach declared dangerous by the Radar Controller), the Navigator told me he was convinced that the Captain might not be able to make a safe landing. I then took over controls unofficially and made a steady approach and landing which was praised by the radar controller.

Conclusion

It was beyond my imagination that the Captain was not aware of the hill on the approach to Runway 26 of Royal Air Force Base Northolt, where he had landed several times. I could therefore never doubt that what he was doing was wrong and dangerous, but yes, when the Radar Controller said we were well below the hill, my reaction to take over and climb steeply was slow by 23 seconds after the instruction had been given.

I am very happy and proud of myself that a catastrophic disaster was averted thereby saving the lives of all on board. Whenever I think of this 'near miss', it sends shivers down my spine. I had been married for only two years seven months and 21 days; my sons were only 1 year 4 months and 21 days old. I am very happy to be living. Thank you, God!

The Board of Inquiry in London UK blamed the Captain. In India the Court of Inquiry blamed the co-pilot.

Yes I never contested, never asked for any awards and least expected to be punished.

Analysis

London Air Miss

It has been beyond my understanding that the Captain, highly experienced pilot with thousands of hours experience and on super constellation, an instructor, with several times landing at RAF Northolt (though not at night), and yet all his approaches declared by the Radar Controller as dangerous.

It has always been on my mind as to why such a situation happen to an experience pilot who has been very familiar with the destination in question, unfortunately this incident was never discussed in the squadron, it always remain question mark with no answers, I have been discussing this incident at various gatherings, friends, socially or among pilot community

I often discuss with my two sons who are senior commanders and instructors in civil airline about the glass cockpit and the automation, my attention was drawn to certain CALL OUTS at certain critical stage of flight that is TAKE OFF RUN and during LANDINGS. Any time if the CALL OUT either on the Take Off run or on landing the CALL OUT by the Co-pilot or Pilot Monitoring is not acknowledged 2nd time by the Captain or the Pilot flying, the Co-pilot takes over controls. This failure to acknowlge by the Pilot Flying or Captain is considered as SETTLE/ SUBTEL INCAPACITATION.

I recall when Wing Commander Terence Joseph Desa who retired as Air Marshal was also on board as a passenger, our flight to RAF Northolt, when learnt about incident/flight he mentioned that it is possible that the Captain was temporally or partially incapacitated.

More than 55 years I had been trying to figure out what exactly was the reason, I think the settle/subtle incapacitation is close to the answer.

Postscript

After retirement I have been trying to contact Flg. Offr. M.J. Eaton to thank him for saving our lives and to invite him to visit India as my personal guest. Unfortunately, I have been unable to make contact even after writing to the Station Commander, RAF Base, Northolt and the RAF HQ. I am very disappointed that even during my visit to London in May 2017, I could not establish contact with him.

THE JWO LASCAR UK COURIER INCIDENT (NOV. 1973) NO. 6 SQUADRON

There was a meeting of old students of Lawrence School, Sanawar (Old Sanawarians or OS) at Bombay in October 1973 which I attended while I was posted at Pune. I met the middle son (Aditya Nehru) of Mr. B.K. Nehru who was then our High Commissioner to the UK. Aditya met me so warmly that I remembered we were never the best of friends at school. We had a lot of fights and I even tried to hurt him on the football field, so I was a bit surprised with his friendly approach. He said, "I believe you have joined the Indian Air Force." I was really taken aback that he knew. I inquired about his elder brother, Ashok, and younger brother, Anil. We departed as good friends, exchanging telephone numbers and residential addresses. I then mentioned that I was flying to the UK in our own aircraft the next month and asked if there was anything he would like to send to his parents. He said he would let me know. Later he called me to tell me that there was nothing that they would like to have from India but would like to meet me. I asked Aditya whether I would require an appointment; he said that they would get in touch. I was quite excited to meet his parents, as I remembered his mother during her visits to the school. She was a very dynamic and impressive personality.

After an uneventful flight from Pune via Palam-Bombay-Djibouti-Cairo-Paris, we finally landed at Northolt London on 9 November 1973. On completion of the formalities, the accommodation for the officers was arranged in the Cumberland Hotel in Oxford Street, while the airmen were put up in a hotel in the Piccadilly area. I had barely settled in, when I got a call from JWO Laskar that his briefcase had been stolen from his room while he was away for just five minutes to help a fellow crew member in the adjacent room. Sqn. Ldr. Bhinder (my co-pilot) and I went to the hotel where they were staying. I met the General Manager and the Security Head and wanted know the action they would take. We then filed an FIR against the hotel management at the nearest police station. The contents in his brief case were his personal papers, his pay book and cash in pounds sterling received from Air HQ as allowance for the trip. Fortunately, the passports of all the crew members were with me. JWO Laskar confirmed that apart from the pay book and some cash, nothing important had been stolen.

There was a message for me at the reception that I was required to meet Mrs. B.K. Nehru at the Indian High Commission on 11 November 1973 at 4 p.m. I met her as scheduled.

Our accommodation in London catered only for bed and breakfast; we were given allowances for meals. Given JWO Laskar's predicament, we decided to contribute a certain amount to him. JWO Laskar turned it down saying that he would manage with the payment we would receive at the Indian High Commission as pay and allowances for the days we are away from our base.

I submitted the requisition with details of the crew members to the accounts section at the High Commission for our payment. The pay clerk (an Indian) refused to pay anything to JWO Laskar till he produced his pay book! I told the clerk the normal procedure that whenever a pay book was either lost or issue of a new pay book was awaited, payment was always made and entries done when the new pay book was issued. I tried to explain to the clerk that we were in a foreign country, that Laskar had lost all his money and he was only asking for what he was entitled to. Moreover, I was guaranteeing in writing that I would have the amount he drew entered in his new pay book. I was most disappointed and angry with his unhelpful attitude. He was least concerned that a fellow Indian had not only lost his cash but other service papers.

I then met our Deputy Air Advisor in London, who happened to be my course mate at the Flying Academy, Wing Commander (later Air Marshal) and informed him about the theft and non-cooperation of the pay clerk. He informed the Air Adviser in the rank of Air Commodore. I was shocked by his solution that the crew members should contribute! I was thoroughly disappointed by his action and felt that one of his duties was to assist Air Force personnel visiting UK. In my anger I told him that we are not here on a holiday. We had come to pick up a consignment for the Indian Air Force and the Air Adviser's office had to ensure that handling the cargo and all administrative support was given to the crew, and also render help if necessary. JWO Laskar was only asking for the payment he was entitled to! However, if the Air Adviser was unable to tell that clerk to co-operate, I would mention this bureaucratic attitude towards the visiting crew to the High Commissioner when I met him on the 15th at his residence for lunch.

That worked! I made sure Laskar was paid. My regard for JWO Laskar went up several notches that while he thanked all the crew members for our offer to contribute, he turned it down. Later, when I was commanding No. 11 Squadron, I was lucky to have him as Squadron Master Warrant Officer.

Postscript

After many years, when visiting my old school at Sanawar along with my wife and staying at Kasauli, I learnt that Mrs. B.K. Nehru was staying in their house there. I called and mentioned that I had met her when she was in the UK. She promptly invited us to visit her. This was in October 2006 and she was 97 years old. She met us so affectionately that we were overwhelmed! When tea and snacks were brought, she poured the tea herself – how she pampered us! She narrated an incident when she and her husband had force landed in a helicopter while he was Governor of Assam and they were missing for two days. Mrs. Indira Gandhi, then the PM, was so worried. We were deeply touched with her gracious gesture. She could hardly walk but insisted on seeing us off to the car. My wife helped her to walk. She has left a lasting impression on us which we can never forget. We learnt the she was a Hungarian Jewish, had survived the Holocaust and had changed her name from Magdolna Friedman to Magdolna Forbath. After marrying Mr. B.K. Nehru she changed her name to Shobha. This remarkable lady died at the age of 108 years at Kasauli. God rest her soul!

Chapter Eight

Leadership and Legacy

AIR HQ COMMUNICATION SQUADRON 1974 TO 1982

Reporting to Air HQ Communication Squadron

After my tenure with No. 6 (MR) Squadron, I was posted to Air HQ Communication Squadron in February 1974. A change of command of the Squadron was also taking place. The Squadron had three types of aircraft on its inventory then: TU-124 (pure jet) and Avro HS-748 (turbo prop) – both these aircraft were being used for transporting national and international dignitaries (VIP/VVIP). The third type was the Devon which was being used by Command HQ (Western Air Command – WAC) for staff visits. The Squadron later acquired an MI-8 helicopter for conveying VIPs/VVIPs to destinations where there were no airfields.

I was excited to be posted to a very highly professional and looking forward to assignment of flying VVIPs. There was a change from piston engine aircraft to pure jet engine aircraft. Palam being close to our parents' home, we could meet them often.

Shock Followed Excitement

One day, when I had barely spent two weeks in the Squadron, all officers were asked to assemble in the briefing room for AOC-in-C WACs address. We could hear the C-in-C shouting with anger! He was livid and said, "My name is mud!" His extreme annoyance was due to an incident involving

Sqn. Ldr. Jerry Sharma. (Thank God, Jerry was not present otherwise given the C-in-C's anger, he would have really hauled him over the Coals!)

Sqn. Ldr. Jerry Sharma's Incident

Sqn. Ldr. Sharma was the captain of the flight to Hyderabad with Prime Minister Mrs. Indira Gandhi on board. A three-night halt at Hyderabad was scheduled. Accommodation for the crew and the Prime Minister was arranged by Andhra State. The entrance to both the accommodations was side by side.

Sqn. Ldr. Sharma called on his course mate, Sqn. Ldr. Clarrie D'lima, who was then posted at the Navigators School in Begumpet. Meeting course mates is always celebration time and since there was no flight for the next three days, both of them had a good beat up session! After the revelries, Sharma returned to the guest house where the rest of the crew were staying around mid-night. It was no surprise that he entered the wrong gate – he walked in where PM Mrs. Gandhi was staying! He immediately realised his error and while coming out saw that the security guard was sleeping. Sharma woke him up and fired him for not doing his duty diligently. Thereafter, he went to off to sleep. He returned to Delhi as scheduled with Mrs. Indira Gandhi on board. He forgot the incident after that.

What he did not know was that in the meantime the guard who had been on duty, believed that the captain of the PM's flight would report him and that he might lose his job; he reported the matter to his superior, the guard commander. The latter too felt that his job could also be at stake, and through the full chain of command the matter went up to the DG Police, Andhra State. Realising that his men could be pulled up, thus reflecting poorly on him, DGP called the Chief of Air Staff and informed him that the Captain of the PM's Flight was seen under the effect of alcohol and was challenged by the guard on duty past midnight. (The guard should have challenged him outside the gate and not inside, and not when going out.)

Without any inquiry or asking Sharma what had exactly happened, he was thrown out of the Squadron and the CAS asked the C-in-C WAC to warn the others.

Hence, AOC-in-C WAC entered the briefing room shouting angrily – *"My name is mud".*

By then we knew what had really happened and disappointed that the matter was not investigated. Sqn. Ldr. Sharma was posted out bringing an end to his promising career. He had been with the Squadron for a few years and had an excellent record. He was highly professional, dedicated, sincere, and a good human being. I believed that all the officers posted to Comm. Sqn. were highly professional and mature and had blemish-free records. However, it was the Indian Air Force that lost a good officer.

My first month in the Squadron! First the welcome I got and the Sharma incident! I was completely disillusioned. It was very disappointing that neither the Station Commander nor the Squadron Commander stood up for one of their officers, that too one with an outstanding record. I made up my mind that if I ever got to command a Squadron, I would ensure that my officers got a hearing, come what may.

My conviction is that a crew member or an officer posted to the Air HQ Communication Squadron is highly professional with a high level of maturity; therefore his statements must be honoured. My later personal experiences of flying with Mrs. Indira Gandhi led me to believe that if the Sqn. Ldr. Jerry Sharma incident had been brought to her notice, she herself would have got the case dropped. She always had full faith and regard for Communication Squadron crews.

President of India Shri Neelam Sanjiva Reddy

It was known in the Squadron that President N. Sanjiva Reddy was a devotee of Lord Balaji and was a regular visitor to Tirupati. It was also known that during flights to Chennai, he would always request that the aircraft circle around the temple. On one such occasion, the Captain was Sqn. Ldr. (later AVM) C.R. Ghosh in a TU-124, flying at 33,000 feet from Delhi to Chennai. Just before approaching over the temple, he found the President fast asleep, Ghosh was in two minds whether to disturb him or not. After consulting the crew, he decided not to disturb His Excellency and the aircraft continued to its destination.

The President woke up and inquired about the circling over Tirupati. The Military Advisor (Maj. Gen. rank army officer) to the President told the captain that the President wished that the aircraft circle around the temple. He was informed that the aircraft had already descended and was only 10 minutes from door open time. The captain also told the MA that as the President was sleeping when the aircraft was over the temple, it was decided not to disturb him. Also, the aircraft did not have sufficient endurance to climb and return for a circle around the temple. After landing at Chennai, the Military Advisor called the CAS that the captain of the aircraft. Sqn. Ldr. Ghosh refused to obey the President (who is also the Commander-in-Chief of the Armed Forces) to circle around the temple.

I was the co-pilot on that flight. We received a message that Sqn. Ldr. Ghosh had been relieved and that another pilot was being flown in. I then sent a message that the President was staying for three days at Chennai and the aircraft was returning without any passengers. Therefore I would fly as captain and Sqn. Ldr. Ghosh could fly as the co-pilot. This was agreed to.

After landing at Palam, we were called by the Station Commander (then Group Captain V.B. Vasist) to brief him about what had happened. After three days, I went as captain to Chennai to bring back the President. The Station Commander received the President and congratulated him on his second life. He explained to the President about the endurance of the aircraft and also told him if the captain had gone back to circle around the temple, it might have led to disastrous consequences due to lack of fuel. However, if the aircraft had survived, the captain would have been sacked for putting the life of the President in danger. President Sanjiva Reddy saw Sqn. Ldr. Ghosh standing a little away. He graciously went to Ghosh and hugged him. The matter was closed.

FLYING VVIPs

Veeaeepee Skvaadran Aadarsh Vakya: Seva aur Suraksha

On one particular flight on an Avro HS-748 from Lucknow to Delhi, Prime Minster Mrs. Indira Gandhi was on board along with her elder son, Rajiv Gandhi. Since the weather was marginal, we delayed our take off. Just then, an Indian Airlines Avro took off for Delhi. Seeing this, Mr. Rajiv Gandhi (who had been a pilot with Indian Airlines) passed a remark that Air Force pilots were scared to fly in such weather. He was politely told that if anything happened to the Indian Airlines aircraft, they would be responsible and answerable only to the families of about 49 people on board, while we would become answerable to the entire nation.

Squadron Motto *Seva aur Suraksha*

Posting to the Squadron of both aircrew and ground crew was done after rigorous screening to evaluate professional skills and sound maturity levels. Thereafter, the Squadron carried out its own training. Only after being satisfied with the performance of each person, was clearance given to fly dignitaries (VVIPs).

It has always been the endeavour of the Squadron to go beyond our motto to ensure that in each flight the VIP was made to feel comfortable. We are also trained to handle any changing situations and make all efforts to meet different requirements of the VIPs as per the parameters and SOPs of the Squadron. I would like to narrate a few of my experiences with different VIP.

The captain of the aircraft receives and sees off the VVIP. During the flight, a senior non-commissioned officer from the catering trade (who has also been trained as cabin crew) meets all the requirements.

Mrs. Indira Gandhi as PM

I had the opportunity to fly Mrs. Indira Gandhi while she was the Prime Minister and extensively during her election campaigns. She was always on time and never failed to greet the crew with a smile. She would always climb the steps briskly, and did not like anyone travelling with her to be late. I remember once while flying to Pune, when we were five minutes to door open time, we received a message from the Chief Minister of MP (then Mr. P. C. Sethi) that he was delayed by 10 minutes. He asked if we could delay our landing by 15 minutes. Since this would be a change in the door open time, we had to inform her and take her approval. All she said was "Do you think a Prime Minister should wait? If he wants to be there, then he has to make sure he is on time".

She knew the layout of the TU-124. The loo for the crew was at the rear and they had to pass through the VIP cabin. I remember once during an election flight when she was changing her clothes, and I needed to pass through the VIP cabin. On my apology, she said, "Oh never mind! Just go". I am mentioning this because she was so gracious that she never made you feel uncomfortable or was never annoyed. On another occasion, on a flight from Srinagar to Delhi, her granddaughter, Priyanka (then 11 years old) was travelling with her. Priyanka asked if she could enter the cockpit. We agreed and she sat with the Navigator in the nose of the aircraft, with the headset on, listening to the conversation on R/T and within the crew. She told us she wanted to be a pilot like her father (she was already conversant with certain aviation terminology). After landing, when I told Mrs. Gandhi that her granddaughter was asking a lot of questions, she promptly said "I hope they were intelligent ones".

During the elections of 1977, we found a marked difference in her – she would rarely smile, looked tired and confused. I remember once an election meeting was held inside the aircraft itself at Nagpur and when questioned for a clarification would say to check with Sanjay. During the flight I once found her sitting with her legs folded, asked her if she would like to rest on a bed? Her response was, "Oh, don't worry, I am comfortable".

During the general elections in June 1980, Mrs. Gandhi flew extensively. Her departure time every day used to be 0500 hours and landing time 2300 hours. Given the driving time and de-briefing, one can guess how much time she would have got to rest. This went on for weeks. I did most of her flights then and found a marked difference from what I had seen in 1977 – her energy, confidence, and pleasantness were back.

She invited all VIP Squadron officers with their wives to her residence for high tea, where she made everyone welcome and comfortable. She spoke to the ladies and told them how highly professional their husbands were and caring. She appreciated the squadron in a letter to Air Chief Idris Latif.

I have flown Sanjay Gandhi too extensively. He was always accompanied either by the Defence Minister, Deputy Defence Minister or the Minister of State for Defence Production. (As Sanjay was not entitled to fly in IAF aircraft) the ministers would remain in the aircraft until he finished his election work. (Mr Sanjay Gandhi, a flying enthusiast himself, died in an air accident on 23 June 1980.)

The King of Bhutan

It was always a pleasure to fly His Highness the King of Bhutan Jigme Singye Wangchuck. As I had flown him a number of times, he recognised me. On one occasion, flying from Agra to Hashimara, he requested if we could fly over the Taj Mahal. I informed the Agra ATC that I would be flying low over the Taj as requested by the King. I then requested His Highness to come to the cockpit, made him sit on the co-pilot's seat and did some low passes over the Taj Mahal. He was so excited seeing the Taj so low from the air that it was quite childlike. After landing, his secretary said the King wished to be photographed with the crew. We were invited to visit Bhutan. In the Squadron when such invitations are extended, we are expected to thank the VIP and politely decline!

During his next flight in which I was the Captain again, I was surprised by his gesture of gifting me a First Day Cover Stamp of his coronation.

Chief of Air Staff Australian Air Force

I was supposed to pick up the Australian Chief of Air Staff from Bombay when he came from Australia by a civilian flight. When everyone was seated in the aircraft, we waited for the VIP. An officer of the rank of Air Vice Marshal came. A few minutes later, he asked me, "Captain, should we?" I replied, "Sir, we will wait for the Chief". He told me not to wait and proceed. I learnt later that he was the Chief. I felt so embarrassed and later apologised. I had thought their air chief would be of the rank of Air Chief Marshal!

Chief of Air Staff Indonesian Air Force

I flew the Indonesian Air Chief to Srinagar for a three-day stay. The very next day we received a message that he was returning to Delhi. We rushed to the airport and learnt that his son, a young Flight Lieutenant in the Indonesian Air Force, had died in an air accident. We really did not know how to receive him and his wife to express our grief. So I decided that the crew would line up to convey our heartfelt grief and shock.

General O.P. Malhotra (COAS)

I had the opportunity to fly the Army Chief, Gen. Malhotra, many times. He came to know that Col. Ratan Singh was my brother. On one of the flights, he mentioned that the Army had been very unfair to my brother who was probably the only Ordnance officer cleared by the promotion board directly from Lieutenant Colonel to the rank of Brigadier, yet he had been dismissed from service on a petty charge. When he was reinstated and demanded his new rank with full seniority, it was denied to him, so he took premature retirement. Gen. Malhotra told me that he always regretted that my brother had not been given his due. After he retired we met at a social gathering and Gen Malhotra did not forget to express his remorse.

Mr. Morarji Desai, Prime Minister

I had flown Mr. Morarji Desai many times. I remember that he had two requirements. One was to bring the temperature to that outside half an hour before landing. Once, while landing in winter, Delhi was about 9 degrees Centigrade – the rest of the passengers shivered! The second requirement was that if the last meal for the day had to be served, it should be at 5 p.m. and comprise dates, almonds, and goat milk. He generally remained aloof and rarely smiled.

Air Chief Marshal H. Moolgavkar

The flight of Air Chief Moolgavkar was always interesting, and to the minute details. The pilot and steward co-ordination, the sequence from the chief strapping himself to the seat, to engine start, to taxiing, removal of flag and line up for take-off. The COO would be at the ATC for co-ordination.

On one occasion during summer month Flt Lt Nanjapa who was flying from right hand seat with Air Chief on Captain's seat. Flt Lt Nanjapa shocked to see Sgt Bachal the steward placing a frozen hand towel on the Air Chief's head, what Sgt Bachal said later after he saw sweat droplets on the bald head of the Air Chief. Flt Lt Nanjapa was certain that he and Sgt Bachal will be posted out to Chhabua (IAF's furthest NE posting) a punishment posting, but on the contrary message from Air Chief's office that Sgt Bachal to be on all future Chief's flights.

Foreign Dignitaries

I also had the opportunity to fly many foreign dignitaries including the presidents of Maldives, Mauritius, the Sheikh of UAE. The Prime Minister of Sri Lanka, Mrs Bandaranaike was so pleased with the flight and the arrangements that she wanted to gift me a tie pin and said I would remember her whenever I wore it. Her manner was gracious and the fact that she was giving the tie pin to me herself, made me accept it. I still have it.

The Last Flight of TU-124 Raj Hans V 642

I had the opportunity to handle the last flight of Raj Hans V 642 (TU-124) of Air HQ Communication (VIP) Squadron to the U.P. Government Museum at Lucknow on 30 July 1981. I went to see the aircraft out of nostalgia many years later. Sadly, I was very disappointed to see it unmaintained.

Eventually, it was a satisfying stay with Air HQ Communication Squadron, except that my wife's health was not good towards end of our stay. My next posting was as Deputy President, Air Force Selection Board, Varanasi.

Varanasi
Air Force Selection Board

After a successful tenure with Air HQ Communication Squadron, I was posted as the Deputy President, Air Force Selection Board, Varanasi, after completing training as an interviewing officer.

The stay at Air Force Station Palam and with the Squadron had been satisfying professionally and personally. Both my sons completed their early education and got admission to the best school in the country – Lawrence School, Sanawar (HP). The only setback towards the end of our stay was that my wife Renu started to keep ill health despite the fact that all medical tests showed that all was normal.

We moved to Varanasi in the beginning of 1982 and by the grace of God, my wife's health started to improve.

Air Force Selection Board, Varanasi is co-located with 39 Gorkha Training Centre (GTC). As three of my brothers were with the 3rd Gorkhas, I was 'adopted' by 39 GTC as part of their family. We started some combined activities. The Centre Commandant, Brig. Kakkar (from 9 GR) was a keen golfer and he included me in their foursome.

My married accommodation and the army hospital shared a common wall, and the commandant of the hospital, Col. Dhiman, was my neighbour. The medical specialist, Maj. Raja Gopal, apart from being an excellent doctor, was a very keen bridge player. We developed a close friendship.

All the doctors of the hospital played bridge and I made up their foursome. The strength of the army hospital was three doctors including the commandant and they always got an additional doctor on attachment from Lucknow. I observed that that every time the attached doctor was replaced by a doctor who also happened to be a bridge player. I asked Col. Dhiman whether it was a coincidence that his requirement for a doctor on attachment had invariably to be a bridge player. To this he related a bridge anecdote: "There was a bridge foursome, all doctors. One day one of the doctors enters his house for lunch. Just then the phone rings so he calls out to his wife in the kitchen that he will answer it. The wife asks if there is an emergency. The doctor says 'yes', three doctors are already there. 'Oh God!

What about lunch, darling?" the wife asks. The doctor replies, 'I told you *na*, three doctors are already there' and tells his wife to have lunch and not to wait. Bridge players are crazy – even if they are doctors!

The relationship between army, air force, and civil administration was very cordial. However, my relationship with the civil administration developed when PM Mrs. Indira Gandhi was to visit Varanasi in a VIP Squadron aircraft, flown by the Squadron Commander. I received a message from the Squadron to be at the airport as they were bringing a parcel for me. On reaching the airport, I found the visibility to be marginal. The aircraft was unable to land and had been hovering over the airfield for about half an hour. The captain told the ATC to get me to the traffic control as he knew I would be at the airport. I managed to help the aircraft to land. The Chief Minister, Chief Secretary, Commissioner Varanasi and other officers of the civil administration were present. I approached the aircraft and Mrs. Gandhi came down the ladder. She saw me and asked what I was doing in Varanasi. She probably recognised me. The civil administration learnt that I was known to Mrs. Gandhi and that I had also assisted the aircraft to land. The commissioner then told me that if VVIP flights came to Varanasi, they would request me to be present. This added to my comfortable and interesting stay at Varanasi.

The Club at Varanasi (Benares Club) was active. I was told of an incident about General Thimayya who was posted at Varanasi as a Subaltern (2/Lt.). One evening, there was a dinner dance at the club. Timmy, as he was known, asked a British lady for a dance. She very rudely told him that she did not dance with niggers. His pride as an Indian and an army officer was deeply hurt. Timmy then just picked her up and threw her into the swimming pool! (The story goes that he was tried by a court martial but found 'Not Guilty' as there was extreme provocation.)

Col. Guman Singh had been one of the most popular commandants of 39 GTC, and I had the opportunity to meet him during his visit to the Centre after his retirement. I requested him to relate an incident we had heard about him when he was the Centre Commandant involving a cabinet minister. I believe Col. Guman Singh resigned after that incident. It was such a great pleasure and honour to have met him; he was an officer of great dignity and honesty.

Group Captain Bhandari, a highly decorated officer, was the President of the Selection Board. As his deputy, I developed a very good rapport with him.

Snakebite

One day, Major Rajagopal, the medical specialist at the Army Hospital in Varanasi, called me at 5 in the morning that the wife of a corporal whom I had referred to him a few hours earlier has been revived after her partial paralysis. He told me that she had been bitten by a cobra and because of the delay in bringing her to the hospital she was already half paralysed. If she had been delayed by even 15 minutes more, it could have proved fatal.

I called the corporal to know what had happened. He was profusely apologetic for telling Major Rajagopal that I had sent him. "As you know, Sir, we sleep on the floor and just close to midnight my wife was bitten by a snake. I did see the snake and I knew it was a cobra. I tried to kill it when my wife shouted to say that she was unable to move the lower portion of her body including her legs. I panicked. I rushed to wake up my neighbour. He told me that while he took my wife to the army hospital, I should go straight to Major Rajagopal's house and tell him that Wing Commander Yadav had referred him. Major Rajagopal then ran in his *pyjamas* to the hospital which was only a few metres away from his house.

"Sir, I am very grateful to Major Rajagopal for saving my wife's life. He laboured for almost four hours. Why I went to Maj. Rajagopal was that I was told by my neighbours that if your name was taken, the doctor would promptly react even at that unearthly hour. There is a general impression in the selection board that your name carries a lot of weight with the doctors. I was told that when a retired sergeant approached you for arranging an oxygen bottle, the hospital promptly made it available just because the request came from you."

(A retired Sergeant whose mother was in the civil hospital required to be put on oxygen and the civil hospital did not have it. When he approached the selection board for help, he was advised to contact me because of my contact with the army hospital. I realised that if she was required to be put on oxygen, it must be an emergency. So I told the hospital to keep the oxygen cylinder ready and arranged a vehicle from our MT section to reach the MH to collect it and rush it to the civil hospital. The Sergeant was told to reach the civil hospital directly to be with his mother. Unfortunately, his mother expired but the Sergeant did tell his colleagues and family how promptly help had been rendered. He wrote a letter expressing his deep gratitude for the assistance.)

Chapter Nine

Mumbai and the People Who Shaped Me

Posting to No. 11 Squadron IAF (14 December 1984)

My posting to 11 Squadron came as a big surprise as I had completed the ground training (MCF) on AN-32 aircraft and was awaiting flying training. I was a bit disappointed as it had been rumoured that I would take command of No. 12 Squadron, my very first squadron, at its location in Agra.

My apprehension was that No. 11 Squadron was being awarded the President's Colours on 18 March 1985 which was just three months away. I did not know its financial condition or resources. Also, I was new to the squadron as I never was posted there earlier. Normally when one takes command of a squadron, he has been in it at some time or, and is therefore familiar with its role, its responsibility, history and some of the officers. Therefore, there was a little bit of concern about managing the Colour Presentation, knowing that even Air HQ Communication Squadron had prepared a year in advance for their Colour Presentation. Yet, at the same time it was a great opportunity and honour to be the recipient.

Both my teenage boys, then enjoying their winter vacation from boarding school, were keen that I keep up with the times. In those days, 'stone washed jeans' were in vogue. My train booking was to Gwalior with a change at Jhansi. My boys strongly advised me to travel wearing stone washed jeans.

The receiving party at Gwalior station found it very difficult to believe their new Commanding Officer's attire and looked at me from head to toe a few times (they couldn't but help compare me with the outgoing CO who was always meticulously dressed)!

I reported to the Air Officer Commanding, Air Force Station, Gwalior, on 14 December 1984 and put on my shoulder the rank of Group Captain. I was escorted to the Squadron by the outgoing CO, Wing Commander P. Kalavar. The ritual of handing and taking over was done with a brief about the Squadron and its role. I was informed that the squadron had a large number pilots coming directly from the Academy so they required additional hours for their operational training. Also mentioned was that some senior pilots had missed their promotion but were devoted and good at their job – flying. Basically, Gwalior is a fighter base and the Squadron had good relations with the station. He also gave me a small brief on Air Officer Commanding (AOC), Air Commodore Denzil Keelor, KC, VrC (Kirti Chakra, Vir Chakra), a hero of the 1965 Indo-Pak War who was commanding the Station. Normally, if he needed to discuss something, he would invariably come to you instead of calling you to his office.

My father congratulated me on taking command of a 'Battalion' (as he called it). I corrected him, saying that in the Air Force we call it a 'Squadron'. He told me, "Make your own judgement, keep your ears closed and eyes open, and be fair and firm. Remember you can never be firm if you are not fair. Know your men and never punish a good worker even by mistake. Mix with them and lead from the front." *Bhai Yaad Rakhna Imandari Aur Hoshari.*

All the officers got together for an informal chat and to get to know each other. I mentioned that within next six months the squadron would have some major events. The impending one was the colour presentation and that too not on our base but at a different station, Jodhpur, which would put extra burden. With experience, I noted that squadrons do not deviate from norms. They follow the routine. I planned to do things our own way My visit to Command HQ was mainly to pay my respects to the AOC-in-C and other senior Command officers. I also made a short visit to the Air-II branch. The SASO, Air Marshal (later Air Chief) N.C. Suri remarked that the squadron was flying a lot but lacked professionally – quantity YES but quality NO!

The Station Electric Officer (my golf partner) was also the station sports officer. I asked him if he could spare the ice slabs kept in the Battery Room to be used when the air conditioning malfunctioned. He agreed.

Ice-cold *nimbu pani* (fresh lime) in the scorching summer was most welcome. We procured three large tubs and four ice boxes and collected 50/60 empty bottles from the Officers' Mess bar. The Officer I/C breakfast room was to arrange the other ingredients for fresh lime. After filling bottles with fresh lime, he was to put them in the ice tubs and offer it to visitors. The cold fresh lime kept the duty crew and those returning from outstation flights satisfied and contented. Visits to the squadron increased.

The Flight Commander was told to ensure that each outstation flight carried an ice box with fresh lime, chilled hand towels, and sandwiches.

After a squadron flight safety meeting one day, I casually remarked that with more than 30 youngsters in the squadron, the commander was having very peaceful nights. The same night I got a call past midnight from some of them. They told me they had stolen the AOC's service car from his house and had a minor accident, and though the damage was not much, the car was not starting. There were no injuries. I woke up the Chief Engineering Officer first to position a standby car at the AOC's residence as he normally began his rounds of the technical area at 4 morning. He (C-Eng.-O) was to recover the damaged car after getting its location. I had to mention the episode to the AOC. He laughingly told me that he too had been naughty when young and had played such pranks. The matter was closed.

I made it practically a ritual to drop in at the bar in the Officer's Mess, once every fortnight. I would also have lunch in their airmen's mess. I would also regularly meet the senior NCOs in the squadron and have tea with them. On one of my visits to the bar I noticed one of the youngsters (I still remember his name – Flg. Offr. Gill) was very quiet and looked distressed. The next day when I enquired about him, the flight commander told me that Gill was under depression as his girlfriend had ditched him. I told the flight commander to programme him with me for a flight. My idea was to build a rapport and find out what was worrying him. In the meantime, I found from his dossier that he had been the recipient of the flying trophy at the Academy. I told him that I knew about his problem him and that it should not deter him from moving forward. He was a flying trophy winner and now I wanted him to do well and get 'B Green' in his initial categorisation with AEB. I told him to forget everything and concentrate on flying. After a day or two, Gill came to my office and told me that he had no girlfriend; the flight commander did not like his smoking and was not happy with him. I then told him I was there for him and he should concentrate on his flying. A day later, he came again and requested if he could be sent for training for AN-32s Aircraft. "Oh shit!" I exclaimed. "The MCF for training AN-32 started a week ago. Why didn't you tell me earlier? Today is Wednesday. Catch the Shatabdi to Agra in the evening and report to the Officer I/C MCF AN-32. They will naturally tell you that the training has already commenced. You should tell them that I, your Commanding Officer, received the message that you should join the training."

I then called OI/C MCF training AN 32. He had been with me in the Communication Squadron. I requested him to accept Gill and that I would request Air HQ to regularise his move and induction for AN-32. Fortunately, the officer at Air HQ who was handling such courses was a friend of mine and agreed. I also mentioned this to the AOC Air Cmde. Denzil Keelor. He appreciated the action. Later, I learnt that Flg. Offr. Gill topped the training. He came to see me after I left the squadron and was posted as Station Commander, Bombay to tell me that not only did had he done well at the training but was also awarded 'B Green' as his initial category.

AWARD OF PRESIDENT'S COLOURS TO NO. 11 SQUADRON AT JODHPUR (18 MARCH 1985)

I was posted to the Squadron on 14 December 1984 and the award of colours was planned for 18 March 1985. The award of President's Colours is a very prestigious event. Though I was happy to be the recipient on behalf of the Squadron, I was a bit under stress as there were only three months to prepare for the big day! Squadrons receiving President's Colours have been known to prepare for almost a year in advance. Besides, the presentation was combined with No. 10 Squadron and it would take place at Air Force Station, Jodhpur.

After assuming command, I was asked to attend a meeting at Jodhpur under the chairmanship of SOA (Senior Officer Administration) of SWAC (South-Western Air Command). The SOA of my Command – CAC (Central Air Command) would co-chair the meeting. All the concerned officers from Air Force Station Jodhpur and SWAC were also to be present. This was a preliminary meeting confirming that the place and the date had been fixed. As the Squadrons being awarded belonged to two different commands, the chair (SOA SWAC Air Vice Marshal P.K. Jain) made a request that both the commands should ensure maximum help financially or otherwise to its Squadron. Air Vice Marshal Rudra, SOA CAC, reacted and stated that as far as CAC was concerned, the squadron can expect no help and that it could generate funds by itself by raffles, etc. I raised the point that I had only three months to prepare. How could I raise funds in so short a time? AVM Rudra got angry and told me to see him in his office at 1100 hrs at Allahabad the next day. The meeting came to an end and AVM P.K. Jain told me to see him in his office before I left for Gwalior. I was terribly depressed seeing my command's attitude. AVM Jain tried to cheer me up by saying that AVM Rudra's anger was not directed at me in particular and that he would extend all possible help. He said, "The reason I have called you is that I learnt that during your posting with Communication Squadron, you had been co-ordinating the Air Force Day Parade at Palam for a few years. Therefore, your guidance will be of great help and I will request AOC, AF Station, Jodhpur, and other related officers from SWAC to honour your advice regarding the parade and other functions. You can always come to me if you feel my intervention is needed." I then mentioned that the education section where the squadron exhibition was to be held was in a very bad shape. The SOA promised that he would have the building renovated.

I reached Allahabad half an hour before the meeting with SOA –CAC and drop in at the Air 2's office and also meet the CPSO (Command Personnel Staff Officer). To my good fortune, he happened to be the PJI (Para Jump Instructor) when we eight pilot officers were posted at Agra. We had become good friends. I told him that airmen's postings are always a sore point for which I would need his help. He agreed.

I landed at AVM Rudra's office on the stroke of 11 a.m. I was surprised that he got up to shake my hand. Before I could apologise for my outburst at Jodhpur, he told me not to mind because it had been meant for the SWAC as they had been demanding pooling of resources which our Command was not keen on. He assured me that the AOC-in-C had promised all possible help. I returned to Gwalior, happy, and confident.

During the next rehearsal at Jodhpur, I met the SOA SWAC and apprised him of the progress and also gave a check list that had been prepared by the then station commander at Palam, Group Captain V.B. Vasist. It had minute details about every item of the parade at Palam; to give an example – the flower pots with a particular plant that were lined up along the red carpet for the chief guest to lead him to the dais each of the 150 plants had to be absolutely identical. If one were to count the leaves, they would probably be the same number in each!

On my advice, one aircraft was attached to SWAC for easy movement of all requirements for the colour presentation.

I called the Nav. Leader and the two flight commanders and briefed them about the meeting at Jodhpur. We formed a co-ordinating committee with Nav. Leader Wg. Cdr. Banga as chief co-ordinator and the two flight commanders, Wg. Cdr. Sukhjit Singh and Wg. Cdr. T.K. Mitra to assist; Sqn. Ldr. S.C. Kumar and Sqn. Ldr. Manaise were also to be part of the committee. It was decided to meet in the afternoon to assess the progress. Wg. Cdr. Sukhjit Singh to take care of operations in case we were not taken off the proposed Command exercise; DAVP (Directorate of Advertising & Visual Publicity) were past masters in organising exhibitions and Sqn. Ldr. Kuma met the Director who promptly extended help by sending 12 experts with their specialised equipment including display boards, cameras, enlargers, and developers. They worked round the clock in shifts. We were able to collect photographs from all the stations 11 Squadron had been posted in the past including the photo taken by No. 4 Squadron of our Dakota shot down by the Naga insurgents. We also managed to get a photo of the first Avro received by our first Prime Minister, Mr. Nehru. Our exhibition was highly appreciated. Sqn. Ldr. Manaise was to organise the liquor for our reunion. We needed authority from our supply depot at Jabalpur to collect the liquor directly from Mohan Meakin at Hindon (Ghaziabad). Sqn. Ldr. Manaise went a step further by meeting the MD, Mr. Kapil Mohan, and appraised him of the Squadron's Colours presentation. Mr. Mohan gifted us a quantity matching our demand as complimentary from him!

Finally, the big day dawned. The Colour Presentation ceremony, the President's lunch and the Air Chief's dinner went off very well. The SOA SWAC personally complimented be that everything had gone off just as planned.

AVM P.K. Jain became very fond of me. He moved as Director Work Services at Air HQ and I moved as station commander, Bombay. My request for funds for renovation of our VIP Cottage was acceded to so promptly; he sanctioned the money directly to the station, bypassing the Command!

No. 11 Squadron Reunion at Gwalior (4 April 1985)

The date for the Squadron Re-union was chosen was 4 April 1985 after consulting the Met. Office for weather. It was also a full moon night. It was formal mess dress for officers – white with miniature medals and wings. Lady wives were supposed to wear yellow saris. The white and yellow mix became a big hit under the full moon!

The chef of Vasant Continental, a five-star hotel in Delhi, was known to one of my officers, Sqn. Ldr. S.C. Kumar. We invited him to visit our Officers' Mess at Gwalior which was then in the Residency. He preferred to bring his own staff. He helped us with the design of the invitation card, the seating plan, and the menus for snacks and the main dinner. (The highlight was the 30-odd varieties of ice cream with funny names – one I remember was named after AVM Rudra and called "Rudi's Nut"!)

The entertainment of the guests was planned by the ladies, and its theme, the dresses, the steps, and stage management were a great hit.

As mentioned, the liquor requirement had already been met, courtesy Mr. Kapil Mohan of Mohan Meakin, who had given us complimentary a matching quantity to what we had ordered.

Flt. Lt. Dubey designed the invitation card, the souvenirs, and our mascot on the cutlery.

We managed to invite most of our veterans and serving 'Rhinos'. A big rhino made of wood welcomed our guests.

There was a large number of officers in the Squadron and so we could give personal attention to each guest. The veterans were thrilled and related anecdotes of the 1965 and 1971 wars, the Dakota days and the Squadron moves from one station to another. The guests enjoyed themselves, most of remained in the final dinner party till 2 a.m. in the morning!)

The C-in-C and his wife, Mrs. (Dr.) Sahni, thanked me for the excellent arrangements and the very enjoyable party. He also mentioned that he was planning to move the squadron to Allahabad.

We had the band from the Punjab Regiment in attendance at the Reunion and they performed superbly. Just when we were giving them gifts, the drummer started playing a rocking beat! It was so spontaneous that the entire Squadron freaked out and then began more dancing, cart wheeling, front rolling, handsprings, and some bhangra steps. I wasn't far behind it was like the celebrations starting all over again. On and on it went, the drummer getting even more excited with the response of the Squadron. When I wanted to do a hand spring someone from behind restrained me. I surprised him by telling that I was the best gymnast in my school, he said you were Sir.

Bada Khana

During our Bada Khana, we organised an air show comprising Sky Divers, Army para drops, low aerobatics by Mirage 2000, Heli dance, and finally close formation flying by three Avros.

Aircrew Examination Board Visit to the Squadron (May 1985)

After the successful President's Colours presentation, my attention was on the AEB (Aircrew Examining Board) visit in May. Having just a month and half at our disposal, I was keenly conscious of the remark of SASO (then Air Marshal N.C. Suri) made earlier that the Squadron lacked quality.

I told this to the Flight Commander (Operations and Training), Navigation Leader and the Squadron Engineering Officer. My aim was to prove him wrong. So step one would be to break away from normal AEB visits. I was confident of full co-operation from Command HQ, and planned for three dedicated aircraft, two for pilot examiners and one for Nav. All route check destinations would be chosen by the Squadron, pilot route checks were not to be combined with Nav. route checks, and no route check would be combined with command task as it was customary. We knew from experience that every time a route was combined with a command task, invariably the offloading or loading party was not available, resulting in the examiner and the examinee sitting under the wings for hours.

I informed our team that the OC AEB, Group Captain P.K. Mani and the Navigation Examiner, Squadron Leader Sandhu had been with me in Communication Squadron and we had flown together many times. Therefore, we could expect full cooperation from them.

As for the squadron, we prepared a check list and the sequence of operations so that the AEB visit was as per our requirement and their convenience.

We knew AEB visits had been conducted at Agra, Chandigarh, and Jorhat. I directed our aircraft to land there the day their AEB departed and to collect the question papers.

Training Flight Commander Wg. Cdr. Mitra was to co-ordinate the AEB visit and hold extensive ground training. He was also to prepare our own question papers similar to the AEB question papers procured from the AEB visits of the three stations.

The Operational Flight Commander, Wg. Cdr. Sukhjit Singh was to supervise continuous training to all the pilots who would appear for the tests. Since Gwalior did not have runway/airfield approach aids, all instrument ratings would be conducted either at Lucknow or Jaipur. Sukhjit was to organise two aircraft to proceed to Lucknow and Jaipur with 10 pilots on board each aircraft to practice instrument let-downs continuously and then change destinations so that all the pilots were familiar with both these airfields. Both aircraft were to carry sufficient snacks, fresh lime and fresheners, ice box; NCE to be on board to assist. This practice was to go on till the Ops Flt Commander was satisfied that all pilots had come up to the mark.

Nav. Leader was to carry out training of all navigators, ground training and if required carry out route practice destination of choice and the AEB.

A handout/questionnaire was prepared covering all details and presented to the CO AEB, the Pilot examiner and the Nav. examiner, a day before their arrival, so that they were aware of every detail, and operational and admin requirement. It also included the list of pilots and navigators for their categorisation – initial, renewal, and upgradation.

The squadron ops room was set-up to co-ordinate, support, and monitor all requirement of the AEB.

After meeting the AOC, I invited the OC AEB for a cup of coffee. We exchanged pleasantries and talked about our days in Air HQ Communication Squadron. I told him that after the ground test was over, the examiners and the flight commander would join us to discuss the flying programme. We would make changes if required.

The pilot examiner mentioned that there was something wrong as in the results of the ground test, everyone had scored above 85 per cent. He was surprised that among them were two pilots who, in more than 15 years, had never scored more than 50 per cent. I enquired if they had cheated. He said he had been present during the testing; he felt that the question paper had been 'leaked'. I told him he could conduct a re-test. The examiner refused but maintained that something was wrong. I then informed him that we had worked very hard to bring everyone to a certain level and that he would notice a marked difference in flying as well.

I then briefed the examiners and since Gwalior did not have proper runway/airfield approach aids, all Cat 2 testing would be done at Jaipur and Lucknow. The ATC of both these stations had already been requested to accommodate our testing.

A dedicated vehicle had been earmarked for each examiner with one officer as liaison and a NC (E) so that their movement within the station was smooth. I also informed that Gwalior was very hot in the month of May and therefore on all flights a NC (E) would be in the aircraft with plenty of fresh lime, fresheners (frozen hand towels) and sandwiches to make the flight a bit comfortable.

The testing went as per plan and timings were maintained. Fortunately, the aircraft behaved and remained serviceable during the entire testing schedule, for which the engineering officer and DSS were complimented. The ATC at Jaipur and Lucknow co-operated fully.

The OC AEB in his debrief complimented the squadron on their performance and graded it as exceptional. More than 50 per cent initial examinees were awarded 'B Green' and the remaining 'C Green'. All the renewals had upgraded their category and instrument ratings.

After our exceptions performance with AEB wrote, Do letter to Air Marshal N.C. Suri and attached a copy of the AEB report to our exception performance. "Quantity Yes Quality Bigger Yes".

Three Aircraft on Ground (AOG) for More Than 3 Years

On assuming command of the squadron at Gwalior, I found three Aircraft on Ground (AOG) for over three years for lack of routable spare parts. The Squadron engineering officer told me that our AOG demand had been pending since long. After discussion with station chief engineering officer, I learnt that 11 Squadron was on the last priority. According to him, top priority was of communication (VIP) Squadron, next was the communication flight of each command – we came last. Moreover, our command (CAC) took away parts from our aircraft whenever their Comn. Flt. aircraft needed the parts. Therefore, our priority was actually on the negative side.

My first action was to stop cannibalising, even if the requirement was for our own aircraft. This was not taken lightly by Command HQ as this was the normal practice (29.92) in all Squadrons of the Indian Air Force. The logic was that there was no harm removing a part from an aircraft that was already on AOG. I decided to break this standard practice even if the C-in C's aircraft was down for want of spare parts. Sure enough there was such a requirement for the C-in-C's aircraft which I turned down. On hearing this, Command did not take it lightly! SMSO (Senior Maintenance Staff Officer) of the command with the rank of an air vice marshal and the AOC (Air Officer Commanding) of my station who was my immediate boss told me of the standard practice, and that they were responsible to see that the C-in-C's aircraft was airworthy always. I was able to convince them that the Com. Flt. aircraft was entitled to obtain parts on priority 2 and till then I would position my aircraft with VIP configuration with VIP qualified crew. In other words, I emphasised "Why take my part? Take my aircraft". I then briefed the staff officer to the C-in-C about my suggestion so that he did not get a distorted feedback. I was lucky that the C-in-C appreciated the Squadron's concern about its routable parts.

Next, I planned to get all the three aircraft on line and make them flyable. I was lucky that the officer at Air HQ level who dealt with allotment of Avro routables was Group Captain E.V. Eshwar who was a colleague of mine during our posting to communication Squadron. I told him about our problem of obtaining spares for three aircraft that had been on AOG for over three years. I told him that with his help I could bring these aircraft back on line. He assured his full co-operation.

My next visit was to the AOC BRD Kanpur. I informed him how the Squadron was suffering due to lack of spare parts. I told him that with his help, the Squadron could bring back the aircraft on AOG and obtain 100 per cent serviceability. The AOC appreciated that this was the first time that a Squadron commander has come to meet an AOC of a BRD for this purpose. I told him that I had brought my EO (Engineering Officer) along with the full list of spares with a fresh demand and that he, Flt. Lt. Chauhan, had earlier served under him. With almost 90 per cent of the battle won, I told the EO to meet the Warrant Officer who actually made the allotments and hand over a Squadron memento to him. Flt. Lt. Chauhan was given 30 days to procure all the necessary spare parts so that we could fly all the aeroplanes. Ultimately, we did attain 100 per cent serviceability. I sent a signal informing this to Command HQ and Air HQ. I also wrote a DO letter to the Group Captain at Air HQ and the AOC BRD Kanpur, profusely thanking them for their support.

The Hockey Match

The place was Gwalior, the year was 1985 and the match was between No. 11 Squadron (Team Captain Sqn. Ldr. Manaise of the transport stream) and No. 7 Squadron (Team Captain Sqn. Ldr. Ahluwalia of the fighter stream). The referee was Sqn. Ldr. Bajwa. The game was scheduled for 1600 hrs. Sgt. Shukla, who was part of the Air Force hockey team, was to prepare the field and brief both the teams about the rules of the game. Chief Administrative Officer Gp. Capt. Manjeet Singh was to provide all the administrative facilities. Spectators were expected to be seated by 1530. Commanding Officer 11 Squadron (me) was to receive the Air Officer Commanding, Air Force Station, Gwalior, at 1545 hrs. and introduce the teams, the referee and Sgt. Shukla to him.

The AOC arrived on time and was duly received by CO 11. He noticed that 7 Squadron ladies were absent and inquired if they had been informed. I replied that the entire station was aware of this hockey match. The AOC had a soft corner for 7 Squadron as it was a fighter Squadron and showed his open bias.

The match was so highly charged that not was only the entire station present, even the Gwalior township people who were associated with the station were there to witness it. It was well-known that the match was 'transport vs fighters' and it was also known that the AOC favoured the fighters, and that created great interest.

The 11 Squadron team was aware of this bias and that made their spirit peak and raised their morale high. Though both the teams were balanced, yet 80 per cent of the time the ball was in the 7 Squadron half.

The first half went goal-less. However, in the second half, 11 Squadron scored a goal in the eighth minute. I noticed that the AOC was pacing by the side of the field, cheering the 7 Squadron team. To emphasise the neutrality expected from the AOC, I placed a fly swatter on the table in front of his chair to indicate 'Sir, sit back and enjoy the game'.

When 15 minutes were left, the 'fighter types' were becoming desperate to score the equaliser. The referee was under great pressure to award a penalty push against 11 Squadron but was helpless as the ball was far from entering the 'D' area of 11 Squadron. (to please the AOC.)

When the ball was eventually within the 25-yard line, a minor foul was committed. The referee awarded a penalty push against 11 Squadron. As per rules, even in a serious foul at the 25-yard line, a penalty push was generally not awarded. At the most, the player committing the foul could be removed from the field.

Tempers began running high. The Captain, Sqn. Ldr. Manaise went into a near-uncontrollable rage. He was so furious that four players had to hold him back. Seeing that he was very angry, I ran into the field to subdue him. In his anger he told me to get off the field. I had to tell him firmly that if you have faith in *Wahe Guru* let them have the penalty push which we will protest. However, as luck would have it, the penalty push did not result in a goal. In the last minute, one more goal was scored by 11 Squadron.

Expectedly, the outcome did not please the AOC at all! He showed his extreme annoyance to the Squadron Commander 7 Squadron, who tartly replied that after pulling 9G, one cannot expect such a performance on the hockey field.

11 Squadron hosted a party in the Officers' Mess that evening to which we invited the AOC and his wife and also all the officers of 7 Squadron with their wives – the 7 Squadron officers regretted their inability to attend. AOC asked me if we had invited 7 Squadron officers and their ladies. "Yes sir, we did, however it seems they are preoccupied." The AOC was disappointed.

This hockey match was the talk of the town for many years.

Chapter Ten

Final Years in Service and Retirement

Air Force Bombay (Nov. 1986 – Feb. 1989)

There never was a dull moment during my Bombay posting – one crisis was followed by another. It was an ultimate test to manage and get through that nightmare, both operationally and administratively.

Some incidents that can be disclosed are as follows:

Class IV Civilian: His Dismissal and Re-trial

I barely got over a hair-raising situation when a new one knocked at my door.

A Class IV civilian was tried and dismissed by a Court of Inquiry for being absent without leave for over two years. The civilian went to the Bombay High Court to contest his dismissal. The High Court observed that his trial had been carried out by a non-competent authority, upheld his plea and ordered that he be re-instated and paid his arrears within three months. He could be re-tried within the same period by a competent authority.

I received instructions from my Command HQ to comply with the court verdict and ensure against contempt of court. Another nightmare!

It became a 'Catch 22' situation. I needed to complete the trial and pay the arrears within three months. Three months of severe tension with the accused not co-operating. However, we managed with advice from the civil administration section at Air HQ.

An Airman Threatens to Kill his Wife

I received a complaint that one airman (rank Corporal) was threatening to kill his wife. I called him, his wife and the president of the Ladies Welfare Club (my wife), and the secretary (wife of MWO Chanran) to be present and also called the Station Adjutant. I asked the airman what he had against his wife. He said, "I have always met all her requirements. I told her that I love her. All I wanted from her was to be quiet when I was eating."

I told the airman, "I have understood your problem. Now you listen to me carefully. There are four types of *bhojans* (meals): one, the food a man cooks for himself is known as *Anand Bhojan* meaning whatever he cooks is pleasurable. Two, a mother cooking for her son is known as *Prem Bhojan*, whatever she cooks is with lots of love and affection. Third, is when a daughter-in-law cooks for her father-in-law; that is *Kuker Bhojan* meaning she serves him whether he likes the food or not, and the fourth, is when a wife cooks for her husband. This is known as *Kalesh Bhojan*, the wife prepares the best of food but won't allow him to eat without cribbing, gossiping, and relating a host of problems." I said to him, "It is not just with your wife, it is with all wives. I have found a solution for myself and you ask MWO Chandran – he too must have found one. When we eat and the wife starts cribbing, we close our ears and concentrate on our meal. It is better you learn this because some day, you might lose your temper and do something you will repent all your life. You can ask all your elders. This phenomenon is universal and we all live with it. Control yourself for at least one month and let your wife expend her cribbing and grouses. Let me know the progress."

At the end of the month came and told me, "Sir I am loving my *Kalesh Bhojan*".

Two Airmen Sharing Accommodation

The amount authorised for airmen's accommodation is so inadequate that even small houses go beyond the sanctioned amount. It is therefore accepted that two airmen share an accommodation to keep the rent reimbursement within the authorised amount. In one particular case, one of the men had to undergo a short course at Pune and the other man's wife had to go to her in-laws' place. It became a unique case and an embarrassing situation, where one airman is away and the other airman's wife has to her ancestral home. The man who was doing the course was uncomfortable with the prevailing situation. We moved the airman to the airmen's billet. After returning from his course, he requested a posting to Nal Bikaner and that was the end of the matter.

I realised we were grossly short of entitled accommodation for our airmen. Construction was pending for years because of some disagreement between the GE and the contractor. Hence we prepared a complete brief to take up with the Command HQ during the C-in-C's visit.

Alcoholic Junior Warrant Officer (JWO)

A JWO who had lost his wife a year earlier and was looking after a daughter of 13 years and a 10-year-old boy. It was brought to my notice that he was suspected of molesting his daughter when drunk. I was very disturbed and angry. I really did not know how to handle this case, and the first thing I did was to move him into the Senior NCOs' mess under observation and ordered a ban on his liquor. When I called him and the children to see me, I noticed the girl was extremely scared of her father. I thought of orphans homes or contacting her father's relatives. A month keeping him under guard, particularly in the evenings, made things improve. I was happy to learn that he had given up drinking totally.

Issue of Dismissal Order to Air Force Officer Posted with Embarkation HQ, Mumbai

Three officers posted with Embarkations HQ are supposed to handle all defence equipment imported. The three of them from the Army, Navy, and Air Force indulged in smuggling on a large scale. The Army and Navy dismissed their officers; however, the Air Force put their officer on suspension. Finally, he was dismissed and we had to handover the dismissal order to him personally. He was then in jail at Nasik. When the Station Adjutant went to Nasik to serve the dismissal order, the officer in question remarked that the Station was in a great hurry to give him the order. He then threatened the Station Commander and the Adjutant that he could easily harm their sons as he knew where they were studying; that really scared us. The adjutant explained that we had been given the task by Air

HQ we were just following instructions. As far as the station was concerned, we had always met his requirement regarding accommodation and payment of pay and allowances. Yet, we were scared and took some security measures.

Naval Exercise with Indian Air Force

While I was officiating commander of MAO (Maritime Air Operation) HQ, it was brought to my notice that naval aircraft tasked to locate and destroy designated targets were unable to co-ordinate with Air Force bomber. They did not rendezvous over the sea resulting in failure.

I called a meeting with the COPO Western Naval Command. I found that the naval aircraft was based at Goa and the IAF bomber was based at Pune. The crews never meet. So, my first advice was that once in a while they met either at Goa or Pune or wherever convenient.

I notice that after detecting the target, the naval aircraft waited for the IAF bomber to be escorted to it while the naval aircraft carried out a holding pattern, perpendicular to the line of approach by the bomber aircraft. I told the crew of the naval aircraft to do their procedural turns and then hold along the track on which the Air Force bomber was expected to reach. I also told the naval crew to install a homing beacon with IN Morse code so that the bomber could home in on it. When this was done, it was a 100 per cent success. We followed when the Maritime Sqn was with IAF.

Receiving Air Force Dignitaries at *INS Kunjali* (Heli Base)

Since I was still officiating MAO Command, I had to receive dignitaries at Bombay (Santa Cruz) airport by air force aircraft and ferry them to *INS Kunjali* by chopper. On one occasion when the Vice Chief Air Force and his wife visited Bombay, I received them at Bombay airport and requested SASO MAO, with his wife to receive the VCAS at Kunjali. The CO *INS Kunjali* raised issues about allowing SASO and his wife to enter the helipad base. I was disappointed to know this. To avoid any future receiving or seeing off our Air Force dignitaries I discussed it with the COPO Western Naval Command and there were no further problems.

Naval Day Review

At the Naval Review 1987, the President of India, the PM, RM, all Service Chiefs and other dignitaries were also invited. The Chief of Staff WNC was then Rear Adm. Vishnu Bhagwat, a friend from my school. I offered him hangar space and duty crew to receive and see off aircraft or render any other specialised help.

I anticipated the constraints of the Navy in terms of accommodation for our Air Force dignitaries, particularly for our Air Chief. After Vishnu Bhagwat assured me of suitable accommodation for the Air Chief but was unable to confirm it for our AOC-in-C, I then recommended for our C-in-C to regret the invitation.

AOC-in-C's First Inspection Visit to Air Force Station Bombay (now Mumbai)

The format for the AOC-in-C's inspection visit had been the same for some years, with minor changes (standard 29.92). During the AOC-in-C's first inspection visit after I took over command of Air Force Station Bombay, after the formal presentation was over I requested the C-in-C's permission to speak. I informed him that the Air Force Station, Mumbai, was totally neglected. To this the C-in- C promptly said that it was but natural that as other stations like Nalia, Bhuj or Uttarlai had very important operational responsibilities. These would naturally demand more attention. I did agree with him but emphasised that they could sustain without certain facilities as they were compact. All facilities were within those stations, whereas Air Force Station, Bombay, was spread over Cotton Green, while our helicopters were at Juhu and Kalina Camp, Santa Cruz with some distance between them.

We did not have our own married accommodation – for officers, we depended on the Navy and for our airmen we hired housing in the civil area. In Bombay (with its high rentals) it was difficult to find suitable accommodation within the sanctioned amount, hence our airmen lived in areas with poor hygienic and living conditions, thereby inter-mixing with civilians. That left a poor picture about the Indian Air Force. I added, "Sir, if I may say, Bombay is India and if you are known with respect in Bombay then you are known likewise in the whole of the country. The Navy does just that." I then requested if an air show could be arranged featuring the famous IAF aerobatic team, Surya Kiran. The C-in-C agreed and when the air show organised, practically the whole of Bombay turned up at Marine Drive to witness it!

I also informed him that our airmen's accommodation at Cotton Green was awaiting completion for years as there was a dispute between the GE/CE MES and the contractor. We at the station were helpless in the matter. The C-in-C understood our problem and was deeply concerned. After he returned to Command HQ, I received a message that during his next visit, the CE MES was to be present.

The CE MES did not attend the meeting. Naturally, the C-in-C was upset. (I learnt later that the errant CE was removed from Bombay and our work began to be given due importance.)

I soon realised that apart from the heli operations to the oil rigs at Bombay High, the other operational requirement would be only during hostilities. Other than that, our main role was administrative but we lacked infrastructure for it. After identifying what we needed, we looked for those who could help. The other requirement was that Bombay was frequently visited by almost all Air Force dignitaries and also retired Air Force personnel needing cancer treatment which was available only in Bombay in those days.

A major immediate requirement was additional vehicles – one 3-tonner, one 1-tonner and a Maruti Gypsy. Putting in a demand for these vehicles in the normal course could fructify in months (if not years). So I directly contacted the DG Logistics (he was commanding 27 ED during the time I was posted with Communication Squadron). His response was prompt and he told us to send a party to collect the vehicles. Another pressing requirement was to get sufficient funds to hire vehicles for visiting dignitaries and for other official visits. For this I spoke to the CLMO (Command Logistics and Maintenance Officer). As luck would have it, we happened to know each other and were good friends. He agreed in principle, and assured us that funds would be allotted shortly.

Arranging suitable accommodation for staff visits and for senior officers was yet another issue that needed to be addressed. The best option was to renovate one of the rooms in the Officers' Mess. To my good luck, AVM P.K. Jain was posted as DG Works – Air HQ. (During our Squadron's Colour Presentation he was the SOA SWAC. I was helped in preparing for the parade at Jodhpur and he had been happy with the way everything went off smoothly.) I, therefore, took the liberty to make a request for funds for renovation of the room. This was promptly agreed to and we were allotted one lakh rupees directly to Air Force Station, Bombay. I could upgrade one of our Officers' Mess rooms to a semi-VIP state.

Personal relations built up over one's service matter a lot!

SPONTANEITY OR RE-ASSURANCE

In Mumbai, I received a call from SOA WAC AVM Choudhary that he needed to come to Mumbai to personally thank me for something I did for retired Wing Commander T.B. Chaudhary. I told the AVM that he was welcome to Mumbai but need not take the trouble to come just to thank me. A day later I received a letter from Mrs. Choudhary that Wg. Cdr. Choudhary was no more and before dying he had requested her to write to me and also requested AVM Chaudhary, his nephew, to thank me personally. She wrote that these were his last words. I could not help but cry.

One day, I received a call from SASO SWAC that a veteran Wing Commander who had retired 20 years ago and was down with cancer would be coming from Kolkata with his wife to go to the Tata Memorial Cancer Institute, Mumbai. By now I knew that anyone down with cancer at that age would require three things – transport, accommodation and fresh blood during surgery.

I requested the station medical officer to receive Wg. Cdr. Choudhary and his wife at the airport and bring them to the Officers' Mess where their accommodation had been arranged. However, on arrival, the visitors had told the medical officer that they had relatives in Navy Nagar and would be staying with them.

The same evening, I received a call from Wg. Cdr. Choudhary that he wished to meet me. Once I learnt that he was CO PTS while I was doing command training on Packet aircraft (C119G), I told him we would come and pay our respects. However, he insisted that he and his wife would meet us at my residence.

After greeting each other and reviving old memories of the Packet days, I noticed that he looked very tense. He sat on the edge of the chair and making gestures to his wife. When he repeated this for the third time, I told him that we had already fixed his appointment with the doctor and had also arranged blood donors of his group. I could see that he was relieved and shifted back on the chair and relaxed.

The station medical officer who had accompanied Wg. Cdr. Choudhary to the cancer institute told me that he has been advised to come after three months for surgery. The station doctor and I went to the institute to find out why the operation was being delayed. The doctor told me that his case was beyond the stage of surgery. In fact, he told me that Wg. Cdr. Chaudhary had very little time left – not more than three months. This came as a rude shock. I told the doctor that Wg. Cdr. Choudhary was not only my instructor but had been my CO. I almost begged him to find a way. He said even if there was any hope of recovery, he would have taken the chance. Have they been told? I asked. 'No,' he said.

I went to see them off at the airport. I knew it was going to be difficult to hide what I knew. He hugged me and smiled. In the letter his wife had written that after returning from Mumbai he felt at ease and happier and had died peacefully.

I really do not know whether I deserved his thanks because he never took any help – transport, accommodation, or blood; still he had thought of me on his death bed. I really feel sometimes that spontaneity or reassurance may be far more than the actual help rendered.

I am a firm believer that God places each person in a place where he has the opportunity to do something good for society. One should never miss that opportunity. Never get intoxicated with the position one holds.

An Admission to Sophia College

Bombay is one city where every Air Force dignitary visits with unique requests/ demands, which the Station Commander Bombay is expected to meet, irrespective of whether he had resources available to him or not. One Station Commander, Air Force Station Bombay (Mumbai) narrates such an experience. For the sake of full disclosure – the Station Commander happened to be me!

The Station Commander was seeing off an AOC-in-C, after his personal visit to Bombay. The dignitary asked the Station Commander if he could get his daughter admission to Sophia College for the Mass Media course. The Station Commander's wife, who happened to be an ex-student of the college, indicated to her husband that there should be no problem. After the wife gestured ok, the commitment was made.

So the very next day my wife and I went to the college and requested if we could meet the Principal and stated the purpose. Knowing that my wife was an ex student, we were promptly seated in the waiting room. My wife was very pleased to learn that the Principal was Mother Braganza, when she had studied there mentioned she was her favorite student.

As the Principal approached the waiting room, my wife whispered that she was not the Mother Braganza who was principal during her time. My wife told the Principal that she was a 1967 science batch student and asked about the Mother Braganza she knew. "Oh, she is my sister and has retired a few years ago. Anyway, what can I do for you? The Principal asked.

My wife said, "Mother, we have come to seek admission for an Air Marshal's daughter". The Principal asked if it was for the Air Marshal who had come with his wife yesterday asking for an admission to the mass communication course commencing the next year. My wife said yes. At this, Mother Braganza got a little annoyed and said that she had explained to the Air Marshal that this course was for graduates which his daughter was not. So, when the entrance tests which are conducted in a group for entrance to the course the applicant could not be present as at that time her own graduation final exams would be on. Under the circumstances, she said, it was just not possible. Saying, "You know admissions are a sensitive issue and we just cannot deviate from the norms", she abruptly left, adding that she had lots of work to do.

We came back very dejected. I believe nothing is impossible. Next morning, I requested the station education officer to find out who was the head of the polytechnic that conducted the mass communication courses and the relationship with rest of the college.

I was informed that the head was a lady, who was very dynamic, learned and tough but reasonable. Also, she known to take decisions independently. I then sought an appointment with her. Wanting the appointment to be of odd time. The appointment was fixed at 1052 hrs. three days hence.

I then requested the APM with his two motor cycles and the jeep to rehearse the time it would take for his two motor cycles, escort jeep to travel from Air Force Station to Sophia College. This was done for two days and Air Force vehicles were within the premises of the college, it caught the attention of the college authorities, the polytechnic in particular. They were told that the station commander has an appointment with the head of the polytechnic and since the time of appointment is fixed, they wanted to know how much time it will require to make it on schedule.

On the appointed day, I entered the college gate at 1050 hrs, took 30 secs to go around the roundabout, 15 secs for the driver to open the door and 15 secs to reach the lift for the head of polytechnic's office on the 3rd floor. The lift was already down on the ground floor. It took 20 secs for the lift to reach the 3rd floor and it took me another 20 secs to reach Miss Mullah's office.

During the exchange of greetings, she looked at her watch and I apologized for reaching 20 secs early as I gained 20 secs as lift was already down. (I learnt later, that Miss Mullah got lift to remain down at 1045 hrs. to facilitate for me be to be on time the pressure had built.)

"Yes, Group Captain, what can I do for you?" she asked. (My tone and my body language displayed totally the opposite – humble, simple and unimportant). "Ma'am, do you have any relations in the armed forces?" I asked in turn. "None," she replied, "but I have great regards for the defense people".

The conversation then went like this:

Self: "You know during wars it is we (juniors) who fight the battles, if you win you are alive but if you lose you are dead. But you know even during peace time we fight battles here - if we win we remain, but if we lose we go home".

The head: "So what is the battle?"

Self: "Well, an air marshal (like a general in the army) has given me a task to get his daughter admitted for the mass communication course with you?"

The head: "Then what is the problem?"

Self: "The girl is not yet a graduate but you know it is not her fault if Darjeeling is a disturbed area and her exams have been postponed. As I understand, one has to be tested in a group to seek admission for such a course but unfortunately during your admission test, her graduation exams will be on, so she cannot be present physically at that time."

The head: "Well, the situation is very tricky". (From her voice I could make out that there was some concern and probably my drama was having some effect in generating sympathy).

Self: "Ma'am I can understand your constraints and as I am basically a farmer, I will go back to farming". (I could see that she wasn't listening but thinking).

The head (after a small pause): "OK, Group Captain, can you give me an assurance that you will produce her graduate certificate by end-January?"

I promptly committed to do so.

The head: "I will waive off her test in a group but she will be tested separately in a 3-hour paper session. You said her exams are in October, we will then call her in end-November. Please collect the forms from the reception and if possible submit the same within the next 2 or 3 days with 2 passport size photographs of the applicant. The exact date of the test will be notified later."

My thank you was unusually loud! I could not but help bursting with happiness. She extended her hand to wish me good bye. I held her hand with both my hands and told her that I just didn't have words to thank her. It had been a shot in the dark but it worked!

I called the C-in-C and requested if he could send 2 passport size photos of his daughter. He asked me three times if I was sure that the college was accepting her application. The same evening, I received the snaps and we submitted the forms the very next day.

The girl arrived in end-November that year and I accompanied her, the air marshal and the education officer to the college. She was given the test paper and we were told leave and return after 3 hours. Being quite tensed up, the air marshal decided to stay. We were then advised to wait in the waiting room.

After he had been pacing the floor for about half an hour, I advised the air marshal that we could play golf at the US Club. The education officer would remain at the college in case anything was needed.

At the golf course, the air marshal just could not concentrate on his game. After the 5th hole, I realized he had lost every one of them.

"Sir, if I may tell you, we have already completed all the formalities for admission and paid the fees", I said, finally putting him out of his misery!

"You b......! You wanted to make money off me!" he exploded.

"Only Rs. 60/-, Sir - 5 holes and a birdie", I replied.

I was posted out of Bombay before the air marshal's daughter joined Sophia College and I learnt later that after passing out of the college, she joined BBC.

Postscript

Twenty years later, my wife wanted us to go and show Sophia College to our grand-daughters. She also wanted to show them the very room where she and their 'Dada' first met. We learnt that the same head polytechnic was still there! We promptly met her and told her how grateful we were that she went out of her way to help us, and that after 20 years we come to thank her. Though she did not remember fully, but was very amused and wanted me to talk to her husband. She told him that here was a guy who has come all the way from Delhi, to thank her for something she did 20 years ago. We had lunch together and had a hearty laugh about the whole episode. Yes, it was a carefully staged drama, but it worked!

It has always my endeavor to try and help; even if it sounds impossible, to at least make an honest attempt.

The head Polytechnic was Ms Mullah.

Mrs. Sharda Mukherjee, Wife of First Indian Air Force Chief and Governor of Gujarat and Andhra Pradesh

During my tenure as the Station Commander of Mumbai, I got a call from Raj Bhavan, Mumbai that I was expected to attend any official function at Raj Bhavan. I found this call odd. I requested my staff to check with Raj Bhavan the reasons for this open invitation.

Citizens from all walks of life are invited to the 'At Home' – para military personnel, industrialists, bureaucrats, politicians, and eminent personalities including senior officers from the three armed services posted in Mumbai.

It so happened that at the previous Independence Day 'At Home' hosted by the Governor of Maharashtra, Mrs. Sharda Mukherjee – wife of the first Indian IAF Chief Air Marshal Subroto Mukherjee, two-times Member of Parliament and ex-Governor of Gujarat and Andhra) was one such invitee. She observed during the party that there was no representative from the Indian Air Force. She brought this to the notice of the governor (then Mr. Shankar Dayal Sharma – later the Vice-President and then President of India). She wanted to know whether invitation had been extended to Indian Air Force officers posted in the Mumbai region.

Mrs. Sharda Mukherjee was told that invitations to defence officers were extended to officers of Air Commodore rank and above, whereas the current the senior-most Air Force Officer in Mumbai was of the rank of a Group Captain. She strongly felt that regardless of rank, the senior-most IAF officer should have been invited as more than just rank, he represented the Indian Air Force in Mumbai.

I felt guilty when I learnt that Mrs. Mukherjee was residing in Mumbai and that we were not even aware of this. More so because she had taken the trouble of finding out who was the senior-most IAF officer in Mumbai.

My wife and I went to invite Mrs. Sharda Mukherjee to visit the Air Force Station and meet the officers and their wives. I also informed her that Air Vice Marshal Shaker has been posted as AOC MAO HQ and that he with his wife would also be present.

Receiving Mrs. Sharda Mukherjee IAF Station Mumbai

I received Mrs. Mukherjee. She made us comfortable and mixed well as if part of us. She was so graceful and down to earth that at no stage did we feel that she had been the First Lady of the Indian Air Force and Governor of two states.

In the Station Commander's office, there was a painting of Air Marshal Subroto Mukherjee. I requested Mrs. Mukherjee if I could take the liberty to request her to autograph it. I saw that her eyes were moist when she did so.

It was a great honour for me to meet Mrs. Mukherjee. A very accomplished lady of that stature, dignified, poised, and so down to earth. Thank you, Ma'am!

(Mrs. Sharda Mukherjee passed away in 2007.)

Chapter Eleven

Giving Back and Reflections

Posting at Air HQ DSA (1989 to 1991)

I was posted from Bombay to Air HQ, New Delhi, on promotion to the rank of Air Commodore as Director, Systems Applications.

My work involved space based projects and co-ordination with the Army and the Navy. The Air Force responsibility was with low orbiting satellites (intelligence gathering), the Army was to look into communications and the Navy for navigation and search and rescue; however, the co-ordination was with the Air Force.

For me it was a great learning as I had to interact with ISRO, Bangalore, NRSA, Hyderabad, and DEAL, Dehradun.

During my visit to NRSA and DRDO, I learnt that one of the scientists was renowned globally and also highly decorated. I requested him if he could spare the time to address the Chiefs of Staff committee, on space. He gladly agreed. He was so unassuming that he came to Delhi on his own expenditure – he did not even ask for a transport to take him to Air HQ. A very simple man with extraordinary knowledge on space. The three Armed Services Chiefs were highly impressed and agreed when he stressed that the future was in space.

I was asked by my Chief to give a presentation to the Chiefs of Staff Committee. I stressed the then allocation of funds for space projects was just not enough and that the Government must be convinced to allot more for space projects. I also stressed the need for a 'Space Command'. I quoted what American President John Kennedy had to say about Space: *"Anyone who controls the sea will control the world but anyone who would control space will control the Earth."*

The other good thing that happened during this posting was that my elder son was selected for the Air Force in the Flying Branch. My younger son opted for the Merchant Navy and joined the reputed Babar's Shipping Company.

As I was heading towards the end of my service, I requested for my last posting to Dehradun to build a house and settle there.

AIR FORCE SELECTION BOARD DEHRADUN

I was posted to Dehradun in August 1991 as Air Officer Commanding/ President, Air Force Selection Board, a posting I had requested as I wanted to build a house and settle there. However, Air Marshal Denzil Keelor convinced me to settle at Gurgaon where he was building his house in Palam Vihar.

The bi-monthly get together over contributory lunch with retired air force officers (an event introduced by my predecessor), was very popular and the retired Air Force fraternity keenly looked forward to attending it. I added that canteen services and the logistics section be opened to meet their canteen and ration requirements as I had decided to do whatever possible to ensure that the retired fraternity was comfortable and felt wanted. We would meet their needs within the resources available. I remember coal was in regular demand as a ration issue, as fire places were a must in large houses in winters.

During my tenure as President, Air Force Selection Board, Dehradun, we worked out the syllabus for induction of women candidates to the defence services and all branches of the IAF.

Air HQ asked me to supervise and co-ordinate relief work in the aftermath of the devastating earthquake in Uttarkashi in 1991. A detachment from Air Force Station, Sarsawa, was positioned at the helipad at the DSOI Dehradun with MI-8 and Chetak helicopters. GOC 14 Infantry Division requested if they could conduct their routine exercise with the helicopters (which had been pending for a long time) while the choppers were in Dehradun. I told him all the choppers were tied up in relief work, but I would check if it was possible at Air Force Station, Sarsawa. The AOC Sarsawa confirmed that the authority already existed. They could come with a days' notice. The army managed to complete their exercise and thereafter enjoyed the hospitality of the Air Force station over beer and lunch.

The Northern Army Commander was visiting Dehradun. On the way from the airfield at Jolly Grant to Clement Town (Dehradun) they had to cross a river, the bridge over which had collapsed. The general's cavalcade found it difficult to negotiate the river. GOC 14 Division requested me if a chopper could be arranged for his departure to the airfield. Actually two choppers were arranged – one for the Army Commander and one for the GOC, so that he could see off the Army Commander at the Division and then be at the airport earlier, to eventually see him off.

A few days later, during the evening function held in honour of the visiting Corps Commander, I was an invitee. The General wanted to know how I had managed to arrange the chopper exercise whereas they had been struggling for last two years. I told him, "Sir, I only co-ordinated". He also thanked me for the choppers for the Army Commander. And that is how our relationship grew with the army!

Air Force Golf Cup

With help from the AOA Air HQ, then AVM Mayor (who sanctioned the funds) and the Sub Area Commander Dehradun (then Brig. Y.S. Kanwar) we organised a golf tournament at the DSOI golf course. We made all the arrangements, including a sumptuous breakfast. The highlight of the tournament was beer with cherries served at each tee off! The participation was excellent with a very large number of the retired fraternity present. Former Air Chief Dilbagh Singh, a resident of Dehradun, declared the tournament open. The dignitaries included Maj. Gen. (retd.) Ranbir Bakshi, MC, the oldest member present.

The golf tournament was followed by an evening function with dinner dance and improvised golf putting for ladies. The evening saw great bonhomie. Maj. Gen. Bakshi's wife (they were both over 80 years old then) kept thanking me and saying that never in her life had she danced and laughed so much.

I recall when I went to invite GOC 14 Division for the Golf Cup he said he would be out of station that day. However, he called the Dy. GOC and told him to extend whatever help we needed for the success of the tournament. (He even went to the extent of saying that unofficially he was handing over command of 14 Div. for that day to Air Cmde. Yadav!). That was the kind of relationship we developed with the Army.

Air Force Day celebrations were to be held on 8 October. While planning the function, I just mentioned that the Sub Area Commander was officially the Station Commander, so we should ask him for financial help for our celebration. I was pleasantly surprised by his prompt response and he sanctioned the amount we had requested

On my retirement I was given a very touching and emotional farewell by all the retired air force officers. Former Air Chief ACM Dilbagh Singh was all praise and joked that he was still 'unlearning' all that I had taught him about golf while he was the AOC Pune and I was with 6 Squadron.

I retired on 31 March 1993 after a very happy and enjoyable tenure at the selection board.

My Surgery at Dehradun

Towards the end of my stay with Air Force Selection Board, I needed a surgery. I was to move to Military Hospital R & R, however I was advised that there is an excellent Doctor in Dehradun and known to be one of the best Urologist in the country. The name of the Doctor is Dr. Manoj K Gupta.

On learning about him I was told that apart for being a good Doctor, he is over 6 feet, athletic body, handsome, plays golf, loves his black label and he is black belt. Vow it will be pleasure to meet him.

After exchange of greetings, notice that half of his note pad was filled with his professional qualifications, and with all the pre-fixes, found him to be humble.

Concerned about his fees, couldn't resist to ask him, 'Doctor Sahib, in a restaurant if one fails to pay his bills he is asked to clean utensils, what will you ask me to do, amused replies with a smile, don't worry come, will find something for you to do'.

After the surgery I was put up in his best (VIP) room and I got away with hosting high tea for his entire hospital staff.

We laded up becoming best of friends.

Acquiring Plot at Palam Vihar

Financially I was in a position to either buy a plot or build a house. To do both would be difficult and the reason to build the house at Dehradun was that I already had a plot there. However, Air Marshal Denzil Keelor convinced me to first buy the plot in Palam Vihar and keep the house building for later.

A property agent found a plot in Palam Vihar a bit cheaper because of its proximity to Chauma village. The agent of the seller was different, so the price or rather the rate, was settled. Thereafter, I insisted on meeting the seller, to which his agent objected. I told him that it is but natural that I needed to see whom I was buying the land from. His agent finally agreed with one condition that there would be no further negotiation of the price. I agreed, and met the seller who happened to be the owner of Archie's greeting cards. When he learnt that I was an Indian Air Force Officer, he told me that his family had migrated to the USA and this was their last property to be sold. As he was leaving the next night, he needed the money the next day itself.

Since I was not supposed to discuss any financial aspect, I mentioned the aircraft he would be flying had a Take Off All Up Weight restriction and the money that I would give him was very heavy as it had been earned with my life 'put on the palm of my hand'. I suggested that he reduce the all up weight for the aircraft to take off! The agent understood me and objected, but the seller was highly amused and agreed to reduce the 'weight'. He left it to me as to how much I was ready to pay. The agent again objected by saying that I could quote a low price! However, the seller was very magnanimous to say that he would agree to whatever amount I suggested. I then asked him to reduce the rate from Rs. 1,000 to Rs. 900 per square yard, to which he gladly agreed.

I had to make the payment within a day and was short of Rs. 40,000. After exhausting all the loans possible and my savings, I landed up at a friend, Vijay Khanna, as a last resort. He was the owner of Kanjimul & Sons, renowned jewellers of Delhi. Though Vijay Khanna was a classmate of my younger brother, I had kept in touch with him and his family and they treated me as part of their family. Accompanied by my wife, I went to him with all her jewellery as guarantee and requested a loan of 40,000. Vijay was prompt with money but angry at me for bringing the jewellery. The fact is I am very grateful to Vijay Khanna that I managed to eventually build a house in Palam Vihar.

The Sketch is Mr Vijay Khanna, by his elder daughter Bhavna
Sent to us by his wife Gita

Epilogue: A Journey Beyond the Skies

MY FLYING JOB AFTER RETIREMENT

Goaway Airline

I retired in March 1993 and realised that all my life's savings would go into the house being built at Palam Vihar. I therefore needed a job to sustain day to day running of the house and the EMI on my loan. The meagre pension would not be enough.

I was lucky to get a flying job with Goaways Airline. Its mother company was UVI Holidays whose Chairman was Mr Wilson Fernandez. I learnt that the Airline was importing an Avro HS 748. After having gone through its documents, I realised that the Aircraft being imported (on Export C of A) was an old one and most of its parts including the engines had outlived their service life. (On extension due for overhaul) Finally the DGCA did not allow the aircraft to be imported.

VIF Airways

I then joined VIF Airways, went for training to Germany on the Dornier F 28. The aircraft was far too expensive and the airline was shut before it could be launched as it was unviable.

Trans Bharat

Trans Bharat was a Charter Company operating Beechcraft 99. It owned by an industrlist and run a retired Indian Airlines Engineer. I flew with this company for 5 years, their regular charters were LML (Lohia family) and the Singhanias.

One day, I received message from the secretary to Mr Anurag Singhania

Director LML and son of Mr L K Singhania that Mr Singhania wished to meet me in Bangalore. A return ticket to Bangalore was on the way. I met Mr Singhania who wanted me to fly their aircraft Beechcraft 200. Please check with my secretary the details of pay and allowances.

Mr Dogra secretary to Mr Singhania spelt out the pay and allowance, the monthly pay would be Rs 75,000/- with a furnished house and a vehicle at Kanpur. But, since the aircraft had been returned to its owners for change of ownership in India, they offered me Rs 50,000/- as a retainer fee. I then told them with a pay of Rs 75,000/-, a retainer of Rs 50,000/- was far too much. I then agreed for only Rs 20,000/- Mr Dogra was very surprised that while the company was offering Rs 50,000, why was I accepting only Rs 20,000/-? I felt Rs 50,000 was not justified. A full year passed but the aircraft could not be imported back as DGCA informed that any aircraft older than 15 years cannot be imported. I managed to convince the DGCA that the said aircraft had been operating within India and that it was returned only for ownership change. Another year passed and now they wanted to raise my retainer to Rs 50,000, but I again refused and agreed for Rs. 30,000.

I wanted to change my Maruti 800 to a Maruti Zen, for which I needed to take a loan. In order to sanction the loan, the bank needed a salary certificate. I made a request for the same to Mr Dogra. He wanted to know why it was required. I told him that I plan to take a car loan of Rs. One lakh for and the bank required it. He confirmed that the certificate would be ready the next day and if he was not in the office the certificate would be available at the reception. The next day I collected the envelope and found it had a cheque of Rs. one lakh. I then spoke to Mr Dogra who said take it as loan is from the company!

After two years lapsed and yet no aircraft had been procured, I told Mr Dogra that the company had been paying me for doing nothing. I therefore requested that I be given some job so that I could justify receiving the retainer. If that was not possible and the aircraft was not likely to be imported, I would prefer the retainer being discontinued; also I would like to return the car loan the company was kind enough to give me. My request was agreed to but they did not accept back the loan of Rs. One lakh as Mr Anurag Singhania felt that the company got away by paying me just

Rs. One lakh and not making them procure a car for me! (A kind gestor not to accept the loan back, how magnanimous of LML)

I would like to quote one particular incident when the Singhania family felt very obliged. One day, I got a call late evening from MD of Trans Bharat that I was to undertake a flight immediately to Kanpur. I told him it was my birthday and I had some very close friends over for dinner so I expressed regret at not being able to fly. Then Mr Dogra called to say that Mr Singhania's mother had expired and requested if I could undertake the flight. Dr RK Seth (founder of Venu Charitable Eye Institute) was the guest at my house that evening. He said please go ahead and take the flight. Renu (my wife) was there to take care of the guests. I took the flight for which the Singhanias were very appreciative and thanked me profusely.

Meeting the Singhania Family

I was once asked to come to Palam Airport to meet Mr LK Singhania Chairman LML who was arriving from on an international flight. He requested me to accompany him in his car to his office in GK II. During the drive he told me that he was happy that I was willing to join the company and that Anurag (his son) was all praise for me. When we reached his office, he requested me to have tea with him and that he made his own tea. His 'tea', apart from being made from the most expensive tea leaves, had a number of other ingredients - almonds, black pepper seeds, cloves, a pinch of dry ginger were all I could recognise. I was quite a concoction but tasted great with a special fragrance and lovely aroma. I thanked him for the tea and he thanked me for joining them.

Deepak Singhania MD LML met me when they chartered the aircraft to Jammu. All he said was that we welcome you to the company and said we have valued your views on retainer fees.

I flew Mrs Deepak Singhania on a flight to Lucknow from Delhi. She came to the cockpit to say hello. On landing at Lucknow where her car had been allowed to the aircraft parking bay, she got off the aircraft, went to her car, told the driver to sit on the rear set and got behind the wheel, and zoomed out! While we were busy post flight, I saw her coming back like a rocket. She came to screeching halt where I was standing. I thought probably something left behind. She got off the car and extending her hand to me said, "Sorry Captain Yadav, I forgot to thank you for the comfortable flight and very smooth touch down. Lucknow is my home town and I am always excited when I am in Lucknow." Then she took off again. Vow! I said!

On one occasion the LML the Singhania turned down the charter of Trans Bharat as I learnt that the Singhania would charter their aircraft only if I was to fly as Captain. The Singhania being their regular customer, the Trans Bharat were too happy to agree their requirement. I felt happy that LML placed confidence in me.

I found the Singhania family very polite and respectful. It is unfortunate that they did not get their aircraft as it would have been great pleasure flying this family.

Golden Year Celebration 1956 Batch at Sanawar Ghora Gali, Murree (Pakistan)

The batch of 1956 celebrated their 50th year of graduating from Lawrence School Sanawar at the Founders celebration in 2006. I was able to convince the Indian Air Force to make a low run over the school during celebration with three fighter aircraft as the school fell within their local flying area. The flypast was a contribution to the Founders celebration from our batch and was a great hit.

Though we had left the school 50 years ago. Everything was still so fresh in our minds – all the anecdotes, the *badmashia* and the lifetime friends we made. It was so nostalgic.

Extension of our 50th Year Celebration to Pakistan

Air Commodore Farooq H. Kiyani (retired Pakistan Air Force and Principal of Lawrence College, Ghora Gali, Murree, Pakistan) attended the Founders at Sanawar and learnt that a retired Air Commodore of the Indian Air Force was part of the batch of 1956. He came up to meet me and after exchanging greetings, invited me to his school at Ghora Gali, Murree (Pakistan). He said it could be an extension of our Golden Year Celebrations.

I accepted the offer. Air Cmde. Kiyani suggested that the best time to visit would be the third week of May, 2007. After consulting my batch mates, it was decided to visit Ghora Gali (Pakistan) from 22 to 28 May, 2007. The official invitation arrived, with a message that the Governor of Punjab, Lt. Gen. Khalid Maqbool (who was also the Chairman, Board of Governors and an Old Gallian) invited our batch for a reception at Governor's House at Lahore on 22 May 2007. The Pakistan Dy. High Commissioner would take care of our visa formalities. It did not come about because we could not leave on the planned day because of a bandh that day in Amritsar.

Visa Formalities

The 56 Batch team proceeding to Pakistan consisted of me, my wife, Dr. Anil Soneja, Dr. Monica Soneja, Mr. Bhupinder Pal Singh, Mrs. Promila Singh, Mrs. Yogindra Singh, and Mrs. Bubbly Mohan.

Fearing wrong attributes to my being seen around the Pakistan Embassy, I requested a friend from the travel business to approach the Dy. High Commissioner, Mr. Afrasaid (also an old Gallian). He told my friend that I would be received at the VIP gate and escorted to his office for coffee. I had requested my classmate, Mrs. Bubbly Mohan, to accompany me. By the time we had coffee, the visas were ready.

We talked about our schools. Both the schools had the same founder – Sir Henry Lawrence, the same motto '*Never Give In*', the same name – and both are located on top of a lush green mountain. The only difference was that we had fought against each other. Mr. Afrasaid said it had been such a pleasure to visit our school at Sanawar several times and had seen the list of gallantry awards winners. He told us we would see a similar list when we visited his school at Ghora Gali. It was a nostalgic meeting of students of two sister schools.

Reception at Wagah Border

On 23 May 2007, we were received very warmly by the Principal, Air Cmde. Farooq H. Kiyani, the president of the Lahore Chapter, Mr. Arif Ghaffar, and Brig. Zaffar Hayat (a Pakistani celebrity). The Commanding Officer of the Pakistan Rangers posted at the Wagah Border held a reception for us.

At Lahore

A grand lunch was organised at the Lahore Club within the Defence Housing Area (DHA) (something like our Defence colonies but maintained like cantonments). Chaudhary Tavir Ahmad, DIG Pakistan Police (also an old Gallian), insisted that we stay in his palatial house with a Moghul type garden (we later learnt that his house and his garden were tourist attractions). We were always accompanied by the school administration and an armed guard.

Reception at Lawrence College, Ghora Gali, Murree (Pakistan)

On 24 May, we left Lahore after an excellent stay with Chaudhary Tavir Ahmad and his wife. On the way we visited Nankana Sahib, had a delicious lunch and were received at the school by the Principal, the three headmasters, – Mr. Arjasab Khan Zafar of the Senior School, Mr. M. Aslam Tasnim of the Prep School, and Mrs. Iaffat Nadeem of the Junior School – along with the Head Boy and school prefects. We were then taken to our accommodation. We were free for the rest of the day.

The next day, we visited the different departments, had lunch with the school boys, and went in the afternoon to see Murree township. A dinner was hosted by the Murree five star hotel, P.C. Bhurban.

On 26 May, a reception was organised at the Islamabad Club over lunch by old Gallians. (I had requested Air Cmde. Kiyani if he could arrange a meeting with the 1956 batch of his school. It was in response to this that the reception-cum-get together had been organised by old Gallians.) The response was so good that they called it historic – and those who could not make it, made sure their wives attended. There were two very interesting personalities, both old Gallians. One was Sardar Aseff Ahmad Ali who was Minister of External Affairs when Benazir Bhutto was the Prime Minister of Pakistan (he is supposed to have given the longest speech at the UN Assembly) and the other was General Shamim Alam Khan (who was superseded by Zia-ul-Haq). I asked the General, "Sir you were supposed to be a tough general; was that the reason you were superseded because Bhutto was afraid of you and martial law?" The General replied he would never have hanged him (Bhutto). Mr. Aseff Ahmad Ali welcomed and thanked us for celebrating our 50th year of passing out from school. He said he had guests at home for lunch but when he learnt that old Gallians were hosting a lunch for a batch from his sister school, he could not help but attend such a historic event. He also said that the spirit among our sister schools was such that if we faced each other with guns in hands, our guns would cease firing. Dinner that night was hosted by the Principal at his residence – The White House.

On 27 May, we visited Panja Sahib at Hassen Abdel, and the Lok Virsa Museum. We were also taken to the Taxila excavations and went around the museum.

On 28 May, we left for Lahore. On the way at Gujranwala, there was a grand reception by old Gallians with banners along the road welcoming us. It was a sumptuous lunch with lots of gifts and a ceremonial send off. We were deeply touched by this gesture. At Lahore, we relished the famous Anarkali kebabs and other non-vegetarian delicacies.

We stayed again at the residence of Chaudhary Tavir Ahmed. Mrs. Tavir Ahmed personally supervised the breakfast – no 5-star hotel could have matched the lay out. When I asked DIG Tavir Ahmed how he could manage such a palatial house and the beautiful garden, he said he was actually a big landlord and owned hundreds of acres of land.

The send-off at the Wagah Border on 29 May 2007 was equally ceremonial, and left a great impact on us. It will remain a great memory all our lives. The Commanding Officer of the Pakistan Rangers gave me a message from Mr. Aseff Ahmad Ali apologising for not been able to see us off at the border.

Attachment with My Village

I have always been very attached to my village, Sadat Nagar. Since childhood, it has been my endeavour to do something for it and therefore after retirement I planned to set up a trust. I had a chance meeting with Dr. R.K. Seth, founder of Venu Charitable Eye Institute, who was extensively involved in eye care. I told him about the poor condition of our region in health/eye care.

At my request, Dr. Seth opened an OPD in the village twice a week that was managed by the Venu Eye Hospital at Sheikh Sarai, New Delhi. However, the magnitude of ophthalmic issues was so great that a need for a hospital was felt. Our family then donated one and half acres of land on which a 30-bedded hospital was built in 1999.

The hospital was named after my mother as Bhagwan Kaur Charitable Eye Hospital, Sadat Nagar. It works 24/7, round the year and within a decade has rendered OPD treatment for over 8 lakh patients and conducted more than 50,000 eye surgeries. It became so popular because of the modern and specialised treatment it offered that people from surrounding districts also started coming there.

The hospital was a pioneer in introducing Community Based Rehabilitation (CBR) for training the visually handicapped to be self-sufficient. We also trained a speech/hearing and visually disabled girl, Uma Kumari that restored her pride in herself and enabled her to become self-sufficient. The hospital also took care of Community Eye Health (CEH) and opened an Eye Bank.

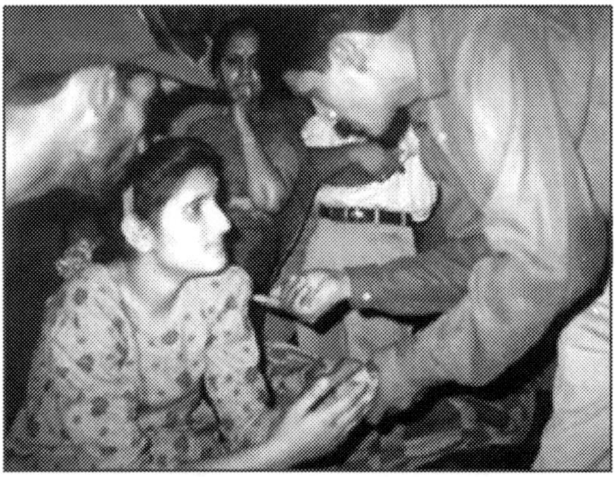

Ms Uma Kumai Deaf, Dum and Blind Trained by our Hospital CBR

Funding for the Bhagwan Kaur Charitable Eye Hospital was initially done by Sight Savers International (SSI). It was so impressed by the charity work of the hospital that it requested their brand ambassador, Ms Debra Winger, a Hollywood film star (three time Oscar nominee) to visit the hospital in 2012. She was highly impressed with the work of the hospital and spent four days visiting all the villages where surgeries had being done. In her press conference, she said she could not believe that such excellent work in modern eye care was provided free in rural India. Ms Winger was also introduced to Uma Kumari, and was happy to see her, smiling and going about her work. Ms Winger complimented the Venu fraternity and the hospital.

With Dr. Seth's help, the charitable eye hospital came up in the village which encouraged me to explore the possibility for a health care facility in the village to cater for the region.

I approached some philanthropists of our country and offered land for the purpose but was disappointed by the lack of response.

I happened to read about Mr. Ratan Tata and Mr. Bill Gates in the *Times of India* of 10 December, 2015 and their concern about nutrition. I wrote to Mr. Tata offering land for a health care centre. I received a prompt response. We organised a visit by an official of the Tata Trust (Ms Archana) and their local consultant (Mr. Vijay Bedi) who came to see its feasibility. This was followed by another visit by a senior Tata Trust official.

Though it did not work out because of some legal issues, I am indebted to Mr. Ratan Tata for his spontaneous and prompt response.

It is my privilege to mention that in memory of my mother, Smt. Bhagwan Kaur, a statue (bust in metal) was installed on 15 January 2019 on the premises of the Bhagwan Kaur Charitable Eye Hospital at Sadat Nagar, District Rewari (Haryana). It was made by the famous and highly decorated sculptor, Mr. Ram Sutar, who also made the magnificent Statue of Unity of Sardar Patel.

Statue of Shrimati Bhagwan Kaur (my mother)

Dr. R.K. Seth, Founder, Charitable Eye Institute

I feel my reminiscences will be incomplete if I do not mention Dr. R.K. Seth, who has contributed towards shaping my character and learning, and his devotion and concern for society.

Having known him closely, I don't think there could be an appropriate word in any language that could truly describe him. Apart from being an eye surgeon, he was a poet, a thinker, a philosopher, a visionary, and above all, a thorough gentleman. Dr. Seth was soft spoken and very humble, dressed simply and was always smiling putting everyone at ease. He was strong of character, with great integrity and honesty.

Meeting him was accidental as I had no plans to settle in Palam Vihar where he was building his house. I had requested a posting to Dehradun where I intended to settle after retirement. However, Air Marshal Denzil Keelor persuaded me to build a house in Palam Vihar (where he was building his). He helped me in locating a plot of land and introduced me to his builder, Mr. Bhusan Munjal. The builder was also building Dr. Seth's house.

Mr. Bhusan Munjal mentioned that Dr. Seth was a noble, devoted and simple person was running the Venu Charitable Society. I requested if I could visit the eye hospital at South Extension.

My very first visit to the Venu Eye Hospital at South Extension was memorable and very educative. I was taken around the hospital and saw that though patients were from different economic backgrounds, all of them were being treated equally with care and affection. I was escorted to Dr. Seth's office and received by him with a hug. The hug spoke much more than words – it transmitted warmth, love, affection and respect, all in one gesture. Later I was to learn that his hugs were magical and meeting him meant a relationship for life with a true friend. I addressed him as Doctor Sahib. "No," he said, "my name is Rajender but you can call me Raj". From Raj it became Raj Bhai and I became Vijai Bhai and thus our friendship blossomed.

Over a cup of tea, I learnt that after experiencing four heart attacks he decided to devote the rest of his life to society. Knowing that every third blind person in the world is an Indian, he resolved to try to remove blindness from the country or at least work towards it. With the blessings of the spiritual Guru, Maharaj ji, and support from his Godmother, Mrs. Veena Singhania, he founded the Venu Charitable Society to provide modern eye care at the door step, particularly in rural areas. He chose a team of dedicated professionals to provide comprehensive eye care which was affordable, accessible and sustainable. I may mention that Dr. Seth was a devotee of Lord Krishna named his project 'Venu' after Lord Krishna's flute.

That 45 minutes with Dr. Seth, soaking in his commitment towards the poor, left a great impact on me and influenced my future life – he was so inspiring and focused.

At our next meeting, I told him about the pathetic condition of our village and the surrounding area and requested if eye care could be provided there. He agreed to visit the village then and there, and saw the undeveloped area. He started bi-weekly OPD by the Base Hospital in August 1992. Operable cases were taken to Delhi for surgery and brought back to the village the next day. Highly impressed with Dr. Seth and his generosity, my father, Capt. Puran Singh, and my cousin, Rao Ram Kunwar, offered an acre and a half of land near the village for a modern eye hospital to be built on it. Dr. Seth had seen the magnitude of ophthalmic problems and promised to build it. (Though Dr. Seth passed away in 1996, Ms Tanuja Joshi, who took over the mission, built the hospital with her personal efforts in 1999.)

The friendship turned into a family affair and on all festivals and birthdays Venu functions also became part of family. During village trips, Haryanvi food was introduced like *Bajra ki Roti, Khate ka Saag, Ghat ki Roti,* etc., which Dr. Seth relished. I still remember him being surprised by the quality/quantity of fresh butter served. My cousin, Rao Ram Kunwar, in whose house the food was served, told Dr. Seth that we serve fresh and seasonal. He added, "I wish we had known you earlier. You could have saved from your heart problems."

Despite his heart attacks and being a heart patient himself, Dr. Seth was lively. He had a great sense of humour. We often just dropped in and joked around. I remember he shared his birthday with Mahatma Gandhi (2 October) and his wedding anniversary was 30 January, so he would joke that his wife Neerja had shot him. We enjoyed his company. His demise was a great loss to the Venu fraternity, his friends and his family and we lost a great human being. I personally lost a true friend.

I can never forget his last day. He called in the evening that he was down with viral fever and so I went to meet him. As I was about to hug him, he said, "Please don't, as you will catch the infection". I told him. "I don't catch infections" and we hugged. He died that night. From that hug I realised he knew his end was near. Every time I think of that hug, my eyes get moist.

He had been working very hard for land to be allotted where he could build a proper hospital and shift from South Extension which was a rented accommodation. Fortunately, land was allotted at Sheikh Sarai during his lifetime. Bhumi Puja was done in 1995 and the foundation stone was laid in 1996, in his presence.

Ms Tanuja Joshi, who had been with Venu Eye Institute and Research Centre since its inception, took over after Dr. Seth's demise and carried his legacy forward. She expanded, modernised, and professionalised the Centre. She has been his true vision, his mission, and his values. Ms Joshi, who works 24/7 round the year, takes no leave. Her aim is to bring up eye care at Venu to world standards and continues to expand. She has been very passionate about care of the elderly and has added a Geriatric Centre. Also, through a 'book club' she is spreading the message of 'ease of ageing'.

Mr Naresh J Kotak (Naresh Bhai) Owners of J M Baxi & Co (Leading Shipping Company)

At times strange things do happen, Mr Naresh J Kotak popularly known as Naresh Bhai, shared ownership with his elder brother and cousin of a leading Shipping Company more than 100 years old spread over the globe bonded with me an ordinary citizen with tremendous social and economic gap. I really cannot call it a friendship, it is the humbleness, simplicity and natural good nature of Naresh Bhai to be friendly, and probably that made him to like me and treated me like his friend. I learnt the true meaning of being magnanimous from him. I had known that he rubs shoulders with leading industrialists of our country and abroad, but with me as an ordinary and as equals.

With Naresh Bahi

It is early 1950s when my wife's father in Okha as the Harbour Master, Naresh Bhai's.

Bhabhi Nirmala Ben (his cousin brother's wife) and my wife's mother out on a walk struck a friendship, thereafter the families remained as good friends.

The friendship strengthen when my wife was studying in Sophia College Mumbai, the Kotak family became the local guardian to my wife and took care of her.

After our marriage I was introduced to the Kotaks when my wife wanted to pay her respect to Ba Naresh Bhai's mother and where I met Naresh Bhai for the first time and bonded over a drink being served with lot of affection and love by his personal attendant Natha Bhai.

We remained in touch thereafter, his responses were always prompt and spontaneous.

Naresh Bhai remained a bachelor and lives in his own a 5 storied building on warden Road Mumbai.

I can never forget his magnanimous gesture when he offered his flat which was locked up over ten years to renovate, furnish it and allow my granddaughter to stay during her training for Air Bus 320 aircraft, after joining Air India, since my granddaughter was given only a day's notice to reach Mumbai, she and her mother were then put up in one of the best hotel in Mumbai with vehicle and a driver till the flat was made ready

I really do not know how could I ever repay. His secretary who was coordinating mentioned to me that Naresh Bhai told him that it is more than 50 years of our friendship and that is least I can do for Vijai Bhai as he always addressed me.

Thankyou Naresh Bhai I am indebted to you for life. Lesson learnt no body is ever too big to be friend with any.

Mera Bachpan

Jai se baris ke pani mei baha kar mushkarate thai
Mujhe kagaz ki wo kisti zara phir se bana dena

Many many years later while lying on my back, eyes wide open but seeing nothing, unable to sleep, mind running wild uncontrolled and the memory of my childhood crept in and wow what a childhood! *Wo badmashiyan*, absolutely raw and fearless, nothing in world mattered. I went into a trance as if I am back there, enjoying the freedom.

My friends always over shadowed my *Kothi (house)* stay. Outside with friends, completely different. It was all fun and laughter, carefree and living in a world of our own. If there was heaven it was this. We were always on the move; even school was fun too! We were disciplined and never punished. The bigger fun was enjoying the wild fruits, BER (*Zizyphus mauritiana* or *jujube*, a thorny plant). It was so much fun plucking the fruit, often stung by the thorn; eat the bad one first to enjoy the good one later. We rarely reached the good ones as by time we finished the sour ones, our lips have become sore. The other adventure was *nimoli* a fruit of Neem. Climbing the tree was no big deal but having *nimoli* was fun. The other exploration was *peel* (Haryanvi grapes), again a big tree found in the forest area. Going to the forest area and witnessing herds of deer was always exciting and *peel* is like the grapes but much smaller in size. These trees are totally extinct, after the deforestation done in our area, and so as the deer have vanished. The other exploration was wild bitter gourd - when it ripens it becomes sweet. More than enjoying the fruit, it was the fun and adventure and to be away from home and be wild. Above all it was getting wet in the rain, jumping into puddles, splashing and making *kishti* (paper boat) and seeing it float and its movement and those innocent smiles with naughty eyes can never be explained but registered in our hearts for ever.

Some Anecdotes, My Village Stay

Pure Ghee, I can never forget one episode. It was then all barter system and pure ghee was the medium or currency. People mostly lived in *katcha* or semi-stone houses with their cattle kept some 50 to 100 metres away from their home in a structure called *Nohra*. The control of the ghee used to be with lady of the house, under lock and key. On one occasion the lady, after melting the butter to make ghee and waiting for it to cool, left for the *Nohra* to attend to the cattle. She suddenly realised that she hadn't locked the ghee and her husband was at home! It couldn't have been more than a minute or two, and she ran back with a stick in her hand, and yelling, "*Pee gayo saro ghee ne*! *En puto mair bhi tho Kona*" ("He has drunk off the entire ghee the bastard doesn't even die"). The husband merely kept lying on *khatiya* (wooden bed) covered with a blanket in the *pauli* (what we call 'lobby' in modern living). She started beating him with the stick, and she didn't have to check - so sure was she that he had polished off at least a kilo! All he had said was "*Godo mai thodi chiknawat ayi*" ("Got my knees lubricated").

Ghee sudhare sag ne badi bahu ko nam (it's the ghee that makes the food tasty but elder sister-in-law law takes the credit) When the elder sister-in-law cooks it is always a celebration as she has control of the ghee. As I was told while having a meal at Srichand's (my friend) house by the younger daughter-in-law.

Jamayi (son-in-law). The other ritual I learnt was that the son-in-law of any family visiting the village is treated as the son-in-law of the village and they pool in all resources to make him comfortable. During meals, all the women of the village sing to entertain him. The songs (*seethna*) are generally naughty and funny and equally the *jamayi* (son-in-law) will answer appropriately. On one occasion the *dal* served was a bit watery so the *jamayi* suddenly got up pulled up his *dhoti* (the dress those days) – the singing stopped and when inquired if there was anything wrong, the *jamayi* said, "*Mai dal ki katori mai gauto maru gau shaiad ek aadho dano mil jayai.*" (I will try and dive into the bowl of *dal*, maybe I will find some grain in it!) Those days such was the friendly attitude of the people that the sense of humour always prevailed!

Rao Lal Singh
For My Learning

During my village stay, my mother asked me to spend some time with my elder sister.

My sister married to Rao Lal Singh's son Rao Mohinder Singh. Rao Lal Singh a big Zamindar of village Sidhrawly Dist. Gurgaon, however they had moved to Haily Mandi near Pataudi Railway Station

Rao Lal Singh was always traveling with about 10 to 15 people. I joined his troupe and enjoyed the attention I started to get. While traveling to Rewari from Pataudi the Station Master held the train almost 15 minutes once he learnt Rao Lal Singh was traveling, and this is where I learnt the extant of popularity and the tremendous respect he enjoyed among the South Eastern Punjab which is now South Haryana or Ahirwal.

Rao Lal Singh never touched upon my failures or try to council, he always spoke to me with lot of affection and love, never try to tell me what is good and what is not, my being presence with him in itself was learning.

Rao Lal Singh a towering personality over six feet always meticulous dressed in snow white Kurta and Chudidar dedicated and a great Leader but NOT a politician. The Chief Minister of Punjab was very keen that he (Rao Lal Singh) fight election which he always turned down, however he helped two politician, to emerged Rao Birender Singh who was adopted to the House of Rao Tula Ram (Rampura House) and Rao Abhay Singh also acquired lot of landed property through adoption to the house of Saharanwas, Rao Abhay Singh a humble, pleasing personality and very honest person. It was believed that the politician of the region during the living time Rao Lal Singh could never win an election without the support of Rao Lal Sigh.

Rao Lal Singh during the riots of 1947 formed a group with fire arms and horses, started to move around saving lives of Hindus in the Muslim dominated area and Muslims from the Hindu populated area, After the Nawab of Pataudi then Mr Iftekhar Ali Khan learnt that Rao Lal Singh has saved lot of lives, to be more affective and faster he placed his armoury and the stable, with that help Rao Lal Singh almost formed like his own army. Because of his swift action there was no blood shed in the region. This earned him tremendous love affection respect among all religion, cast and his popularity to the extent that there was no geet folk songs sung by ladies during all rituals, festivals and private function without his name being mentioned.

The Nawab Pataudi wanted to facilitate by offering a massive Kothi (house with 100 acre of land on the Pataudi-Pataudi Railway Road, which he turned down, he thanked the Nawab for the kind gesture and told him it was just an idea to save blood shed but it worked.

I may mention that the legacy of Rao Lal Singh is being carried forward by his Grand Son Major Ashok Yadav by providing quality education in the rural area so that they can compete with their urban bias.

Village Chitadungra (Dist. Mahendergarh)

My frequent visit to my maternal uncles place were enjoyable, interesting but also distressing.

My Mother's great grandfather owned thousands of landed property which got distributed as the family were growing, my four maternal uncles were left small land holding but sufficient for them to sustain. Being a bhanja (maternal nephew) I was treated like a prince, but their fights over petti things were disturbing, though they would always put up good front and the maternal aunts would sit with me while I would have my meals.

I always loved going to my maternal uncles place but retuned distressed.

YEARS ADDED TO MY LIFE THE FAMILY LEGACY

I am proud to mention that the legacy of our Ancestors is being carried forward by our future generations that 'Bado ka aadar karo aur unka kahana mano' (respect your elders and listen to them)

It is therefore creditable of our family to be unaffected even when we are living in a time where the moral fabric of our society is getting impregnated with decaying value system and ethics

I have passed on the safe guards my mother advised control 'GREED and ANGER'. I have added safe guards against TRIUMPH and TRAGEDY - both are dangerous, one leads to bloated ego and arrogance and the other leads to depression and withdrawal.

Even if I sneeze both my sons land up to find out if I am OK; and if I sneeze louder, then my grandchildren too show up. What a great feeling to be cared for so much! My younger son Capt. Anuj Yadav lives in his own accommodation, just a 10-minutes' walk away. He was a senior Captain (master) at sea with Bergesen Shipping Company and changed his profession to become a Pilot and now is a senior commander with Indigo Airlines. My elder son Group Captain Monish Yadav, a fighter pilot, part of the Air Force Aerobatic Team, is the only pilot who during the Kargil Conflict of 1999 to successful fire the Laser Guided Bomb LGB) on Tiger

Group Captain Monish Yadav, Hero Kargil War, 1999

Hill, while flying the Mirage-2000. He took premature retirement to fly with Indigo Airlines. He too lives in his own accommodation just 10 minutes away by car. Capt. Shreya Yadav my granddaughter, daughter of my younger son Anuj, Pilot with Air India flying the Boeing 787 (Dream Liner). Rhea Yadav my other granddaughter, daughter of my elder son Monish, undergoing training for issue of Commercial Pilot Licence. That makes three generation of Pilots.

My grand-daughter (Capt. Shreya Yadav) escorted for Phera

My children and grandchildren always doing something that make our hearts swell with pride. The compliments keep pouring in. Whether in class room or in flying, the performance have been excellent and highly professional acknowledged by teachers and equally by flight instructors.

We as grandparents are very fortunate to be present at wedding of our first granddaughter Shreya my younger son's daughter. The wedding spread over Goa, Hyderabad and Delhi was meticulously planned and executed. There were anxious moments and apprehension for being a love marriage.

After meeting our grand son-in-law Capt. Anirudh Reddy was found to be very humble good looking and professionally very sound a pilot with Air India also flying the same aircraft as Shreya the Boeing 787 (dream liner). As our granddaughter described to us about her in-laws to be of very good nature not only that she liked them very much but she said anybody would like them. Both side parents are extremely happy with the marriage, and we as grandparents in our twilight years can never ask for more.

We are very lucky by God's grace that we live very close to our children and for a break we move to Dehradun for few months in defence Colony which is lush green with no pollution.

My golf 4sum at Gurgaon and Dehradun is identical, jovial, and like-minded and enjoy playing together. Privilege to name them, at Gurgaon Air Marshal K S Chaturvedi, Air Marshal Gautam Nayyar, Lt General Raghu Saharawat and Group Captain V K Kukerja. The 4sum at Dehradun are Col. K S Mann, Col B M Dara and Col. K S Manhas.

I am also happy to be giving some time and contribute to the Venu Charitable Eye Institute, provides best eye care in Delhi region and rural area with its satellite hospitals.

Having said above sure adds years to my life.

To Sum Up My Journey

The following words of silver screen legend Sophia Loren probably sum up my journey:

"When I got enough confidence the stage was gone.

When I was sure of losing I won.

When I needed people the most they left me.

When I learnt to dry my tears I found a shoulder to cry.

When I mastered the skill of hating, someone started to love me.

While waiting for the light for hours, I fell asleep the sun came out.

No matter what you plan, you never know what the life has planned for you.

Success introduces you to the world, failures introduces world to you.

Always be happy, when you lose hope, God is there to tell you:

friend it's only a bend and not the end."

It is destiny which will determine your path/journey.

And the journey continues....

My Mother My Inspiration